T0208403

Battling Addiction,
Bondage and
Temptation

Battling Addiction, Bondage and Temptation

THE WAR BETWEEN THE
FLESH AND THE SPIRIT

Darrian T. Cobb

Library of Congress Control Number: 2020922819
ISBN: Hardcover   978-1-6641-4298-5
               Softcover   978-1-6641-4299-2
               eBook   978-1-6641-4300-5

To order additional copies of this book, contact:
Xlibris
844-714-8691
www.Xlibris.com
Orders@Xlibris.com
821645

Contents

Contents

About the Author

I can remember the first night that I was ever exposed to an addiction that I still battle with to this day. I was ten years old, and I was hanging out at one of my friend's house. We were doing what most ten-year-old kids did, playing video games until three o'clock in the morning, eating pizza rolls, prank-calling people we knew, just living the stress-free life with no other cares in the world. But very vividly, I remember my friend at the time, late at night, going to a website on his laptop. Out of curiosity, I wanted to know what he was looking at because he looked very intrigued at what he was watching. That night, I was exposed to pornography, and the seed of lust was planted in my heart for years to come. I soon started sneaking and watching pornography at home, behind closed doors or when my parents went to sleep or whenever I was home alone or had the chance to. I always watched it, which would then lead to me masturbating. This habit of mine transformed into an addiction in a matter of one month that lasted for years. The seed of lust had taken root in my heart, and I could not go a day without lusting over other women or having explicit thought run through my mind.

Fast forward four years later, I was exposed to another addiction that I still struggle with to this very day. I was fourteen years old, hanging out with a couple of friends from school one day. We were just hanging out as usual, listening to music, scrolling through Instagram, Facebook, and Twitter, trying to keep up with the latest gossip and telling one another the latest news or even gossip around our school. Then suddenly, one of my friends pulled out a vape pen and started smoking while he was talking to me. I had no clue what it was that he was doing, nor did I know the effects it had on your body. When all my friends started explaining what it was and what it did, I felt like I did not belong. Yes, I was the odd the man out of the group. I was different, a square, as what some people might have called me. My amazing parents raised me to know what is right and what was wrong, even my grandparents helped raise me from time to time, and they taught me everything that I know about life to this day. But that day I disobeyed my parents and grandparents. I gave up what I knew was right to try to fit in and be accepted by the people I was around. I let the people at the time pull me into an addiction that has had a death grip on me since the age of fourteen by letting them tell me "One time isn't going to hurt anything," "Stop being lame," "It's not going to kill you," "Your parents won't even know you did it." When I tried it, when I inhaled the smoke that tasted like blue raspberry, I felt a feeling that I have never felt before. The buzz, the head high that I felt, felt amazing. I soon fell in love with the drug that is in majority of vape pens, which is nicotine. Soon after that, I would do anything to try to get a vape pen or even get the drug in my bloodstream. My addiction got so out of control I started lying to get it. I stole to get it. I manipulated people to get it. I did whatever I had to do to get my hands on nicotine. Before I even knew it, I found myself transitioning from vape pens to black and milds, cigars, chewing tobacco (dip), hookah, and nicotine pouches. I couldn't function if I didn't have the drug in my system. I couldn't focus if I didn't have the drug. The buzz that I always got gave me a thrill. I loved getting my fix of nicotine every chance I got. The buzz was my escape. It was my way out when I started feeling anxious or nervous. The buzz itself calmed me down and gave me peace, which at the time was in place of God. This addiction to nicotine that I battle with every day is an ongoing battle, but through Christ, he gives me the strength that I need to beat this addiction every day that I wake up.

If you are reading this, I understand wholeheartedly what you are going through. I know what is like to be in chains of bondage that is holding you down mentally. I know what it is like to be addicted to a substance that feels like you can't seem to shake loose from. I know what is it like to depend on a substance or a habit for peace, happiness, or joy instead of God filling those places. I know what it's like to feel shame or condemnation and feel unworthy of even coming to God about your problems. You are not alone in this battle, I know your struggle, but most importantly, God knows and sees your struggle, and all he wants is to be invited into the addiction that you are struggling with.

The day that I let God into my addictions, everything changed. Yes, I still struggled, and I still fell off the wagon again and again and again. But the God we serve is so patient with his children. God eventually delivered me from the addiction, and I now walk in total 100 percent freedom that he has called me to live.

God is bigger than your failures, he is bigger than your addictions, he is bigger than your pain, he is bigger than your depression, he is bigger than your anxiety, he is bigger than your relapses, and most important of all, he is bigger than your sin. It is never too late to bring your problems to the Lord, and you are not too far gone for the Lord to fix. Those are all lies from our enemy, the devil. God loves you so much that he sent is one and only son to die for you and your sins so that you may have a relationship with him.

I hope and I pray that this book pierces your heart, transforms you, and that at the end of it, you can fully trust God with your addiction, experience deliverance, and live a life in freedom which our God intends for you to live. If our Lord and Savior can cleanse me, forgive me, and use me to share my testimony and guide his people to him or back to him, he surely will do it for you. God bless you. You are in my prayers.

Intentionality

To get the most out of this book, I want to encourage you to read it every day, even if it is for a few minutes or one chapter. Growth does not just happen overnight. Growth comes from intentional small steps every day. The more you intentionally want to grow, the more growth you will experience as the days go on.

Mirror

In order to see value in yourself, you must add value to yourself. Pursuing growth and freedom from the addiction or bondage that you are wrestling with will be enhanced by reading this book every day. Most importantly, I want you to visualize yourself beating the things you are struggling with, visualize yourself beating this giant that is in front of you, visualize yourself breaking the chains of bondage that has been holding you back from purpose and a relationship with God, and visualize yourself breaking generational curses that may run in your bloodline.

Modeling

It is very hard to grow or see transformation when you try to do things alone. As human beings, we were not created to be alone. It is not good to do life alone. The Lord himself said, "It is not good for man to be alone" (Genesis 2:18). I want to encourage you to read this book with your friends, girlfriend, boyfriend, wife, people in your Bible study groups, or anybody who you know of struggling with addiction or is in bondage also.

Contribution

Once you complete this book, you then have the tools and the guide to beat the addiction you are struggling with. Not only you, but also the people who you read the book with will have the knowledge and wisdom to share to others what you did to beat your addiction.

Battling Addiction, Bondage, and Temptation: The War Between the Flesh and the Spirit

Growing up as children, all of us have seen an addiction or bondage of some sort in our families, passed down from generation to generation. Not only that, but also who we choose to surround ourselves with can determine what habits we pick up, what addictions we choose to have, or what chains of bondage weigh us down because having bad company ruins good morals (1 Corinthians 6:12 NLT). For some us, unfortunately, we were exposed to it at a very young age by friends or a trusted family member, and the sad part about this is it wasn't our fault that we are addicted to the thing that we are addicted to. It only takes one time for the seed of addiction to be planted and take root in our hearts, which then has the power to control our lives and create bondage.

First things first, what is an addiction? The *Webster Dictionary* defines addiction as a compulsive, chronic physiological or psychological need for a substance, behavior, or activity having harmful physical, psychological, or social effects on the body. Addiction affects our spirit, mind, and body. Addiction can essentially have three different effects on us as humans: spiritual effect, mind effect, and body effect. A spiritual effect is when we ultimately replace God as the center of our lives with something or someone else. A mind effect is repeated patterns of poor decision-making, which makes the addiction stronger and disrupts our thinking. A body effect are the consequences from our poor decisions that can cause stress and anxiety. Research from doctors using SPECT and MRI scans show how addictions can rewire our brain circuitry.

Whether it be a substance (nicotine or tobacco, pills, illicit drugs, etc.), marijuana, alcohol, pain killers, having sex, pornography, an attitude, gluttony (binge eating), greed, pride, lust, lying, shopping, exercising, plastic surgery, gambling, or social media, all of us can be or have been addicted to something that fills the spot in our life where we feel most insecure to self-medicate ourselves from the reality of life's let-downs or even past trauma. Addictions can be for many things: to feel good (a feeling of pleasure or getting high), to feel better (to relieve stress or anxiety), to perform better (at a sport, working out, or even sex), and to satisfy curiosity resulting from peer pressure. What is your escape route? What gives you a way out from the stresses of life? What do you do to self-medicate the pain or the loneliness that you are experiencing? What gives you that temporary thrill of excitement? What helps you focus? Take a moment, write down the things that may bring you comfort or things that you may go to when you begin to become stressed or anxious. It can even be something that you feel you can't go a day without.

Throughout this book, we are going to beat the ongoing battle that addiction has on you mentally and spiritually, which then eventually creates bondage. The first and the most important step to beating an addiction and receiving deliverance from a problem that you may be wrestling with is *being honest not only with yourself, but also with God.* God cannot fix or help us when we are not being 100 percent honest with him. Yes, God already knows everything about you; he knows your weaknesses, he knows your addictions, and he even knows the number of hairs on your head (Luke 12:7 NLT). But the God we serve is a gentleman; he will not just come into your life and help fix what he is not invited to.

In Revelations 3:20, NLT, Jesus says, "Here I am! *I stand at the door and knock.* If you hear my voice and open the door, I will come in and eat with you. And you eat with me." This verse in itself is very powerful and should bring all of us some comfort and trust in our Lord and Savior. He sees our problems, our addictions, things that we were exposed to at a young age, us willfully partaking in the addiction that we know we need help with, in chains of bondage that we may have put ourselves in, yet he is so gracious, so loving, and so caring that he is willing to knock on the door of our lives and sit, help, comfort, and even hear us out as we open up to him about our problems and needs. *But the question is, will you invite Jesus into your life to fix the problems that you struggle with?* I want to challenge you today to let our Lord and Savior Jesus Christ into the addiction or problems in your life and have a conversation with him, no matter how far gone you may think you are. The addiction is not bigger than you, but you are bigger than the addiction! Not only that, but also *the Lord is bigger than the addiction, and through Christ, we are all more than conquerors and can accomplish or beat anything in this life that comes our way through our Lord and Savior Jesus Christ* (Romans 8:37 NLT).

Prayer: Heavenly Father, I confess I have a problem. I need you in my life, and I invite you into my heart and my life today. I want to sit with you in communion and discuss my addiction and problems with you. I admit that I can do nothing, and I cannot beat my addiction on my own without you. Strengthen me during this battle and help me grow my faith and trust in you. In Jesus name, Amen.

Chapter One

IDOLATRY

When you think of the word *idolatry*, what comes to your mind? Biblically speaking, idolatry is the worship of an idol or cult image, being a physical image, such as a statue, or a person in place of God. In other words, idolatry is the worship of something or someone other than God as if it were God. In today's time, no, we may not worship statues, buildings, or other people, but we do worship other things as if they were those things. These things can be broken down into two categories: substance addictions and process addictions. Substance addictions involve chemicals. Common examples of these are alcohol, nicotine, caffeine, marijuana, cocaine, heroin, and prescription medications. Process addictions involve our behavior. Common examples of these are gambling, pornography, shopping, or exercise. If you do not fall under these categories, other examples may be your job, attention from other people, manipulation, money, work, your friend group, approval of other people, or gossip. *My question to you today is, what have you been putting before God in your life?*

Do you know who Ronda Rousey is? If you don't, she is a female

UFC fighter who used to be the champion of her weight class. As one sports analyst said, "She found a definition of herself, and she really liked what she found." At one point in her career, she had to defend her champion belt against another fighter named Holly Holm. The unbeatable Ronda Rousey was beaten and knocked out that night and lost her belt. Her life then spiraled into deep depression. She said, "What am I anymore if I'm not this?" She lost her identity. Why? Throughout the Bible, people are seen worshipping idols. When we begin to worship things other than God, we end up losing ourselves and identity to the thing that we are worshipping.

In the Ten Commandments, God's first commandment is "Have no other gods but me" (Exodus 20:3 NLT). Yes, the God we serve is a very loving God, but he is also a very jealous God. One of God's names in the Bible is El Kanna, which means jealous God. In Exodus 20:5 NLT, God says, "You shall not bow down to them or worship them; for I, the Lord your God am a jealous God." You may be asking yourself, "Why would God be jealous? Isn't it bad to be jealous, vain, selfish, or suspicious?" Yes, it is, but this is another kind of jealousy, a holy version. Why is this a fitting jealousy? Why is God right to want us exclusively for himself? Because he made us, and in Christ, he purchased us (1 Corinthians 6:20, 7:23 NLT). Divine jealousy is not motivated by greed or selfishness. God's holy jealousy is rooted in a desire to protect, provide, and bless. He always and only wants what is best for his chosen ones. And what can be better than his perfect love?

Instead of imagining the negative and hurtful jealousy displayed by a pretty schoolgirl, we need to imagine the protecting and providing jealousy of God. Picture God more as a loving father who discovers his homeless son sleeping in a filthy gutter. Imagine how this father might jealously seek to rescue his son. The father's goal is to restore his son's life, not to further punish him. When God freed the Israelites from slavery in Egypt, he took them to Mount Sinai. At the foot of the mountain, God told them they would soon be surrounded by neighbors who were devoted to other gods. He warned them they would be tempted to turn away and be unfaithful.

However, he assured them he would not stand idly by and allow that to happen. As a jealous God, he would fight fervently for their attention and affection.

When God calls himself jealous, it is a reminder to us that our worship cannot be divided. The greatest commandment is to love God with *all* (not part of) our hearts. He alone is worthy of our devotion. He alone is deserving of our hearts. He knows that the ones he loves will find life, ultimate meaning, purpose, and joy nowhere else. He knows that he alone always seeks what's best for us. He also knows that he alone is the one place where our hearts will find their true home. This is why Jesus came, to remind us that we cannot serve two masters (Matthew 6:24 NLT). He told us that whoever is not for God is against him (Luke 11:23 NLT). It is tempting to be "sort of," "sometimes," or "mostly" devoted to God. But we either give ourselves to him or we give ourselves to other lovers. God is jealous for our love because he is zealous for us to know his.

God, through his word, connects these two concepts of addiction and idolatry. Ultimately, addiction is a spiritual and idolatrous issue. First, addiction and idolatry both occur when something or someone other than God has power over us. When we're addicted, we give more value or importance to something or someone than it deserves. Nothing other than God should have ultimate power over us. Second, addiction and idolatry happen when something masters us. When something or someone dictates our behavior, we might have fallen into addiction and idolatry. We also might deliberately change our behavior to be acceptable to someone. These are also signs of addiction and idolatry. Third, addiction and idolatry take place when we worship or glorify something other than God. Where do you spend most of your time—social media, work, school? What does it feel like when someone takes your phone away? What do you spend most of your money on? What do you give most of your energy or effort to? All these questions can be helpful in discerning an addiction or idol.

Thinking back to what we defined an addiction as in the opening pages of this book and combining it with today's biblical definition, here's a fuller definition of addiction: pursuing something other than

God in a repetitive, habitual, or patterned way to get our needs met and bring us comfort, even though it's harmful to us. When you face adversity or stress, what do you run to? Where do you find relief or comfort? Your answers may reveal your idols and addictions. To get a further understanding of what idolatry is and how God feels about it, I want you to study Ezekiel 14:3-8 NLT, which says, "Son of man, these leaders have set up idols in their hearts. They have embraced things that will make them fall into sin. Why should I listen to their requests? Tell them, 'This is what the Sovereign Lord says: The people of Israel have set up idols in their hearts and fallen into sin, and they go to a prophet asking for a message. So I, the Lord, will give them the kind of answer their great idolatry deserves. I will do this to capture the minds and hearts of my people who have turned from me to worship their detestable idols.' 'Therefore, tell the people of Israel, this is what the sovereign Lord says: *Repent and turn away from your idols and stop all your detestable sins. I the Lord will answer those, both Israelites and foreigners, who reject me and set up idols in their hearts and so fall into sin, and who then come to a prophet asking for my advice. I will turn against such people and make a terrible example of them, eliminating them from among my people. Then you will know that I am the Lord.*"

What God is saying to us here is that if we have any idols that are set up in our hearts, to repent and turn back to him. Doing so, he will forgive us and restore us of everything that we lost. But first, it requires us truly letting go of the things that are in his place. The question you need to ask yourself at this moment is, "What are the rivals for God in my heart and life?"

I hope this chapter showed you the things that may be higher than God in your life and that you let them go and let God in your heart instead. I am praying for you.

Prayer: Heavenly Father, I repent from the idols that I have set up against you in my heart. Forgive me for putting the things that are of this world higher than you. Drive from my heart anything that captures my attention more than you. May I not make you jealous anymore after today by being unfaithful. In Jesus name, Amen.

Chapter Two

CHAINS

The main question that you should ask yourself when trying to tackle or beat an addiction/bondage is *"Do I want to be free?"* Majority of the time, the battle with addiction or bondage is not the fact that the trials are too hard to beat or that it's uncomfortable or painful even, *but do you truly want to be free from the things that you are struggling with?* In John 5:6 NLT, Jesus asks a man who has been lying sick for eighty years, "Would you like to get better?" But what happens when we truly want to be free in our heart but the prayer that we prayed didn't work? What happens when you're reading your Bible every day and still see no transformation? What happens when going to small groups or Bible studies and talking about your problems with other spiritual friends didn't work and you're still struggling to break free from what has you bound? In this chapter, I want to talk to you about "choosing my chains."

What is it that you are continually, intentionally, deliberately doing that you know is wrong yet you keep doing? What is taking the toll on you mentally to the point where you can't even look at yourself in the mirror? What are you choosing to keep doing that is driving you away from God? See, *the addiction or bondage does not push God away from you, but the addiction or bondage can actually push you away from God.* There is not a day that goes by that God does not long to come after you, to love you, and to talk to you. Many times we think God wants nothing to do with us because of our mess, ugliness, or addictions, when in reality, God is actually attracted to your chains/ weaknesses. What if I told you that your addiction, problems, hidden secrets, things that you feel ashamed of, or your chains are the exact things that God wants to use to bring his name glory and elevate his kingdom? Sometimes our God is so gracious that he will actually use our situations, our brokenness, and our chains to set somebody else free.

When we begin to see the things that we are addicted to or our problems, we have a habit of blaming others or even questioning "Why me?" "Why would God allow me to go through these things?" "If I never would have been hanging around these people or at that friend's house, this never would have happened to me." We even start blaming ourselves and say things to ourselves like "If I just didn't ever do that, I would be fine"; "If I just wasn't so curious, I wouldn't be going through this"; "If I was just cool enough or pretty enough, I wouldn't have to try and do things to try and fit in for other people"; "If my best friend didn't betray me, or if my boyfriend/girlfriend didn't lie to me and cheat on me, I wouldn't have to be having sex with multiple people to feel loved"; "If I felt loved at home, I wouldn't have to post pictures of my body on social media to feel approval or confidence in myself"; or "If I just wasn't born this way, everything would be just fine." There are some of you who are probably reading this and questioning why you are going through the specific things that you are going through. Just for a second, zoom out and try to look at the bigger picture. Think how God would think. Try to change your perspective into the perspective of our Heavenly Father. Look at yourself the way God would look at you.

The chains and the bondage that you are experiencing are not about you. God is using some of you to break generational curses off your children and your children's children. There are things that you struggle with right now that your children and your grandchildren will not have to struggle with like you did because you were willing to suffer for it, you were willing to embrace your chains. In Philippians 1:12 NLT, the apostle Paul says, "What has happened to me has actually *served to advance the gospel*." In our eyes, our addiction/bondage counts us out from the promises of God. We think there is no way that God could still use us or look at us the same because of our habits. The way that God looks at us, the way that God sees us, the way that God thinks about us *are not* the same way we look at or see ourselves. In Isaiah 55:8 NLT, the Lord says, "For my thoughts *are not* your thoughts, *neither* are my ways your ways." You may see brokenness, but God sees wholeness; you may see yourself as unworthy or not enough for God, but God sees a daughter or son worthy of his love. You may feel ashamed or bound, but God sees his son or daughter set free by the blood of Jesus.

Now that we know how God feels about us and sees us, what about people? What about our friends, family, or Bible study group? The thought of the people we care about finding out the things we struggle with behind closed doors scares all of us. If people knew you were addicted to pornography, pills, anxious thoughts, alcohol, or anything, all of us would feel a heavy shame. We would feel like we are trapped in bondage because of the thought of what other people may have to say or what they think about our addiction or situation. We think to our ourselves, "If people look at me or think of me in this way, why wouldn't God look at me the same way?" In this exact moment, stop what you are doing and write down WHAT DOES IT MATTER? It can be in a journal, in a diary, in your iPhone or iPad notes. It can be your screensaver, so when the opinions of others about your struggles or your addiction begin to bother you, always remember and say to yourself, *"What does it matter?"*

What does it matter that people judge you? What does it matter that the people you try so hard to seek approval from have negative opinions about you? The fact of the matter is not everyone is going to like you. You can do everything right, and some people will still find a reason not to like you. You were not created for people to like you or to crave the opinions of others. People cannot give you what God can give you. People's opinions mean nothing when you compare them to God's. People cannot complete you like God can.

Where you are at right now in your life is exactly where God intends for you to be, even in your mess or if you feel like you are in the wilderness or if it feels like God has left your side. God *promises* to never leave nor forsake you (Deuteronomy 31:8 NLT). God is with you in your highs and your lows. God is with you in the dark place. God is with you until the day you leave this earth and after. I know this is probably messing with a lot of your theology or things you thought about God. Many times, when God is trying to bring out the things he put inside of us, he has a habit of putting us in heated situations or hard situations. He has a habit of putting his chosen people, his anointed people, his children in what most people call *the wilderness*.

You see, God put people he used in very powerful ways in the Bible, in a wilderness season all throughout the Bible. Even our Lord and Savior Jesus Christ was led into the wilderness by the Holy Spirit. In Matthew 4:1 TPT, it says, "The *Holy Spirit led* Jesus into the *lonely wilderness* in order *to reveal his strength* against the accuser (the devil) by going through the ordeal *testing*." He also does the same thing with the apostle Paul in the book of Philippians. Paul says, "Knowing that I am *put here* for the defense of the gospel." Paul was in prison, in literal chains suffering. Like many of us, Jesus and Paul did not choose to be in the wilderness or in prison. They did not choose to struggle; they did not choose to go through the things that they went through.

People may have exposed you to the addiction that you are fighting, you may have been around the wrong crowd, you may have made bad choices in your life, *but it is no accident that you are experiencing what you are experiencing; God makes no mistakes.* No, God did not give you the addiction or current struggles, but he knows everything that is going on in your life. You have been put in the current environment, state, or struggle that you're currently in so that God can bring out the purpose he placed inside of you.

There comes a point in our life when we need to start saying, "There's a lot of things that I wouldn't choose, but there's nothing I would change." There are a lot of us today who are in situations that we wouldn't choose. No one wakes up one day and chooses addiction; no one chooses bondage, no one chooses hurt, and no one chooses betrayal. What if, maybe, the heartbreak from someone you loved, the betrayal of a best friend, you being introduced to alcohol or drugs or pornography at a young age, the anxiety, stress, or worry that you struggle with is needed to get to your blessing or your purpose? What if the weakness that we experience is needed in order to get to the strength? Write this down in your journal or notes: I AM NEVER REALLY IN CONTROL.

Nothing in our lives are ever fully in your control, from friendships to the people you date, even your addictions. When we date people and hope and pray that they are the one for us to get married to, when we set these goals in our mind for our future, if it's a career or a state we would want to possibly live in, when we have this group of friends that we think we like, we're in a comfortable place. The problem with comfort is that *there is no purpose*. In Proverbs 19: 21 NLT, it says, "People may plan all kinds of things, *but the Lord's will is going to be done.*"

In order for God to get you to your purpose and everything that he has called you to do, it requires God removing the things that hinders you from getting there. When we lose the things or people that we thought we would have forever, when people we love hurt us, when plans that we made without God fall through, nine times out of ten, as humans, we want to cope with that pain. *That can be through watching pornography, having sex with multiple people, drinking, using tobacco, using any type of substance, spending money that you don't have on things, lying, bragging or overweening, or anything else that you may do to cope.* Instead of letting God fill the voids where we are hurting at, we turn to *temporary fixes*, which is where addiction comes in, and then eventually, bondage occurs.

But take heart in this: God knows about everything that you are doing or are experiencing. He knew everything you would ever do when he created you and called you to the purpose that he has for you on this earth. God will use your pain; he will use your addiction, he will use your bondage, he will use your story and testimony to bring his name glory and elevate his kingdom. *Everything always works out with God.* God is so good and so gracious to us and loves us so much that he uses everything we go through to make our lives better while we are alive on this earth. In Romans 8:28 NLT, it says, "We know that God causes *everything to work together for the good* of those who love God and are *called according to his purpose.*" It is not too late for God to use you or forgive you; you are not too far gone, and you are not too much for God to handle. Those are all lies from our spiritual enemy, the devil. If you are alive, breathing, and reading this, God has a purpose for your life, and it is not over until he says so.

It may look like or feel like you're chained to the thing or the person or the thought that has you bound. But actually, the things that you are struggling with are *actually chained to you.* If it takes you being in a season of isolation, relapsing on the addiction that you once broke, getting betrayed by your best friend, not getting your dream job or getting accepted into that school, but you are free in your mind, you feel at peace, you are free in your spirit, and you are now starting to seek a relationship with God and your purpose, *consider it all joy!* I would rather you be hurting and seeking God's face and his purpose for you than you being comfortable and well-off, thinking you have life figured out and that you don't need God. In his presence, there is *discovery.* In his presence, there is *change.* In his presence, there is *revealed truth.*

Take a moment to write this down in your notes: EMBRACE THE STRUGGLE. The things that you are battling have to do with your purpose. It may not be comfortable, it may not be your preference, it may bring you pain, and it may drive you to tears. Before the blessing comes, there will always be trials and tribulations with some suffering. In 1 Peter 5:10 NLT, it says, "After you have *suffered* for a little while, he will *restore, support, and strengthen* you, and he will place you on a firm foundation." The suffering, storms, chains, or bondage are not forever. *If God be for you, no one can be against you, including yourself.* After you've been through the fire, after you have suffered, after you feel like you cannot go on any longer, God will restore everything you lost in that season, whether it be time or people. He will support you in all that you do and will never leave your side. He will strengthen you so that when he exposes you to your purpose, you will be ready to battle or conquer anything that is standing in front of you. You will know how to stand firm with the confidence needed to fulfill the things that he has called you to do.

Now let's talk about *CHAINS*. I want return to the questions that is in the first paragraph of this chapter. What happens when the prayer that we prayed asking God to deliver us does not instantly work? What happens when you're reading your Bible every day and still don't feel or see any change? What happens when you do everything right and obey what the word of God says but still see no change? Yes, God has the power to instantly remove any kind of trouble, addiction, or bondage that is present in our lives. But if he immediately removed them, delivered us, or healed us, there would not be any growth in our character or in our faith/relationship with him, and possibly, no purpose would be birthed.

We would feel like we wouldn't need God, or worse, we might stop depending on him. In 2 Corinthians 12:7-8 NLT, the apostle Paul says, "*So to keep me from becoming proud I was given* a thorn in my flesh, a messenger from Satan to torment me and keep me from becoming proud. Three different times I begged the Lord to take it away. Each time he said 'My grace is all you need. My power works best in weakness.'*" Yes, God hears your prayers; he sees your bondage, and he can see the tears coming down your face. But God knows if he was to take our problems away instantly, he wouldn't hear from us anymore. He is not ignoring your prayers; God is allowing affliction, hurt, and pain so that he can mature you and strengthen you gracefully.

Take a second to write this down in your notes: INSTEAD OF ASKING
GOD TO REMOVE THE CHAINS, ASK GOD TO USE THE CHAINS. If God has
not removed something from your life after you ask, it is for a reason.
As stated earlier, God didn't put the chains on you; he didn't bring the
addiction in your life, and he didn't put you in bondage. *The devil and
life did.* The choices that we make and people we surround ourselves
with did. Things *out of our control*, like being born into a family that
struggles with an addiction or a problem, being introduced to it by
trusted friends, or us accidentally seeing something that we weren't
supposed to see, none of us chose the things we battle with, but
if they are not changing yet, instead of repeatedly asking God to
remove them, ask him to use your situation, struggles, or hurts to set
somebody else free or to bless them. What is more important than
the addiction or the bondage is our response in the middle of it. All
of us have the ability to make choices. Are we going to give up and
give in to the enemies' lies, or are we going to humble ourselves and
allow God to do what he is trying to do in our lives and become a
product of his amazing grace? God always gives us a choice to make
every day we wake up. *God's intentions for your chains are good. But we have
a very real spiritual enemy, and his intentions for your chains are evil.*

Like God, our enemy, the devil, offers us choices as well. The
enemies main goal is to steal, kill, and destroy your purpose. He
knows that all of us are called by God and have a specific purpose.
He knows our potential and how powerful we really are. So what he
does is he offers us a *choice* every day as well. Like me, you were maybe
exposed to some of the things that you battle with today at a young
age. You were with friends hanging out, and they start watching
porn, or one of them is smoking (cigarettes or weed), or one of them
starts gossiping, or they are drinking liquor, or they are having sex.
And if you say no to the peer pressure, they call you names like "gay,"
"lame," "a Debbie Downer," so to fit in, you do things that will help
you feel accepted. In that moment, all of us have to make a choice,
the right choice or the wrong choice.

Eventually, the choices that we make don't just stay choices;
they become *habits*. The one choice to watch porn out of curiosity

can soon turn into a habit of you watching it every day, leading to masturbation. The one choice to try weed just to see how you felt high now is a habit because it's hard for you to focus without it. The one choice to have sex because people were making fun of you or assumed that you were gay because you were waiting until marriage now is a habit, and now anyone you find attractive, lustful thoughts come into your head, and you visualize what the sex would be like. You had one drink while spending the night at your friend's house in high school, but now, out of habit, you have to have a drink or a glass of wine to feel relaxed or calm.

Also, it isn't just about a substance or sex or porn. Some of us have a habit of gossiping, tearing others down, or talking bad about them when they are not around. Some of us have a habit of lying or manipulating people to get the things they want. Some of us have a habit of spending money we don't have on things to try and impress others. Some of us have a habit of comparing ourselves with other people and their lives, stealing our own joy. Some of us have anger in our hearts that has been built up over the years, caused by people hurting us or setbacks or failures. *There is no sin that is greater than the other; all of us have specific sin that we struggle with.*

After our choices become habits, they then become *automatic.* You used to have to make a choice before you watched porn or before you poured yourself a drink. You used to have to make a choice before you cussed somebody out or talked about somebody when they weren't there. You used to have to make a choice before you went and slept with that person or went and bought something to make yourself feel better or use the substance that you are addicted to. But now you don't even have to think about doing it; it just comes to you automatically because you've been doing it for so long. Now it's just what you do to get your way or your fix or your high. Then after you do it, you feel ashamed of yourself because you want to do what is right, but then you ended up doing the opposite, a lot like the apostle Paul. In the book of Romans, he says, "I want to do what is good, but I don't. I don't want to do what is wrong, but I do it anyway."

I can personally relate to this, and this itself is what creates the bondage. The fact that you want to do better but don't is because of the chain that has formed is now automatic, and because of shame, you don't even want to do the thing anymore, and you can't even look yourself in the mirror. It's like anything you try to do to get away from it doesn't work. You are not alone in feeling those feelings.

Before long, the choice that turned into a habit that then became automatic then becomes your *identity*. You begin to identify yourself as the thing that you are struggling with. "I'm a slave to fear." "I'm a slave to pornography." "I'm a slave to my own thoughts." "I'm a slave to the substance." "I'm a slave to the opinions of others." This is where the enemy begins to tell you that you are what you are addicted to or your bondage. He lies to you and puts things in your head that are not even true about yourself. He tells you that you're too far gone, that God can't use you, that God would never forgive you. *If you are reading this, I want to personally tell you to stop believing the lies of the enemy. You are a child of God, and he loves you beyond comprehension. There is nothing that our Father would not forgive you for. As a matter of fact, there is nothing that you can do to make God stop loving you.* In Romans 8:38-39 NLT, the apostle Paul says, "I am convinced that *nothing can ever separate us from God's love.* Neither death nor life, neither angels or demons, neither our fears for today nor our worries about tomorrow. Not even the powers of hell can separate us from God's love. *Nothing in all creation* will ever be able to separate us from the love of God that is revealed in Jesus Christ our Lord." At this moment, no matter what you are going through, rest in the fact that God loves you, no matter what happens or what you do.

Now the choices that became a habit which then became automatic which then became the thing you identify yourself as becomes your *nature*. Whatever it is that you're going through, you now are around people who have the same motives, the same likes, the same mindsets, or even the same addictions as you. You think that all because of your CHAINS that this is who you are and that is just how life is supposed to be. You begin to think that there is no more hope, no chance for change, no chance for forgiveness, and every day you live in the bondage that the chains have created, which all started from one choice years ago. At this moment, write down the names of people *whom you trust,* and sometime today or this week, talk to them openly about this. It is never good to battle things or have to fight/go through things alone. True healing comes from opening up about your problems and then having friends who do not mind praying for you and the things you struggle with. In James 5:16 NLT, it says, *"Confess your sins* to each other and *pray for each other* so that you may be *healed.* The prayers of a *righteous person* is powerful and effective." If you are a parent reading this and you feel comfortable, talk about this with your children if they are old enough to understand; true healing never comes from keeping things in.

The enemy uses our chains for evil because he knows the gifts that God put inside of us. He knows that if we were to ever get free and realize who we really are, that we would be a danger to him and his demons and can make hell tremble. He knows things about us that we don't even know about ourselves. He knows that some of you could be a chain-breaker in this generation. I'll put it this way: *The devil never attacks anything that he is not threatened by. If you are reading this and are being attacked by our enemy, count it all joy! All this means is that you are special to God and you have a very important role in his kingdom.*

Some of us have been chained to anxiety, toxic mindsets, toxic relationships, addictions, lust, depression, or anything else for far too long. Today, if you are reading this, *I speak freedom, I speak deliverance, I speak breakthrough over your life in the name of Jesus.* In John 8:36 AMP, Jesus says, "If *the son makes you free,* then you are *unquestionably free."* If you have been born again (baptized in water in the name of the Father and the Son and the Holy Spirit), it does not matter if you have been chained to something ten-plus years; in the eyes of God, you are his child. When he looks at you, he does not see your addictions or bondage; he sees his child who needs help and whom he wants to use. God knows what you are going through is hard, he knew what would happen, and that's why he factored all of it in by his *grace* into your purpose. In Romans 5:20 AMP, the apostle Paul says, *"Where sin increased,* [God's remarkable, gracious gift of grace [his unmerited favor] has surpassed it and *increased all the more."*

Just like the enemy tries to keep us chained to sin, *our Heavenly Father keeps us chained to grace.* As a child of God, *he will never give up on you,* no matter how many times you fall short of his standard. He is always there pick you up when you fall down. When you try to run away, he will come after you. Everything you have been through, all the pains, all the failures, all the setbacks and the bondage, God is wanting to use all of it to tell a greater story of grace. *I am a number one example of the grace of God. All throughout this book, every chapter and every sentence that I write, I have experienced the things that I am writing to you about.* I want God to use my chains to break you free from whatever you are battling with. I pray that you won't have to keep going through the things that I went through.

Today make the *choice* that you're going to let go and let God use you for his glory. Once you make that choice, it's going to turn into a *habit* of you always spending time with him and seeking his face and his plans for you. Then the habit of you spending time with him turns your actions and your ways into his ways and his heart *automatically,* you won't have to think twice about serving him or helping others. Eventually, you begin to see and *identify* yourself as a child and servant of God who's always wanting to do his will, and it will become your *nature* to want to be like Christ is everything you do. Will you let go to serve God and let him gracefully use you for his purpose and his kingdom? Which CHAINS are you going to serve? I am praying for you.

Prayer: Heavenly Father, you know all my chains and scars. You know all my bad decisions, my addictions, and my bondage. Today I let go of the past and the things that I can't control, and I give them to you. Forgive me for making my problems and my bondage bigger than you. I repent and I wholeheartedly want to be used by you. Use my chains for your glory. Transform me, change me, and renew me in Jesus name, Amen.

Chapter Three

DEVOTED

When it comes to choosing to beat an addiction or break free from the mental bondage that holds us down, an essential part of that process is being devoted to not only being set free from your chains, but also being devoted to God and the purpose that he has spoken over our lives. First things first, what does being devoted mean? The *Webster Dictionary* defines *devoted* as "having a *strong love or loyalty* for something or someone." Being devoted is a *daily* choice that all of us must make in order to get to the things that God already has planned for us. Yes! I did say *planned*. Long ago, before any of us were ever born, God saw each of us individually and *set us apart to be used by him in a specific way*. In Jeremiah 1:5 NLT, God says, "I knew you *before* I formed you in your mother's womb. Before you were born *I set you apart and appointed you*."

No matter where you are at in life or in your walk with God, our Heavenly Father has amazing plans for you. Whether you are close with God or you are far away from God, *his plans do not change*. There is nothing we can do to mess up his plans for our lives. He knows exactly *what* he wants to do, *when* he is going do it, *how* he is going to do it, *who* he is going to use, and *why* he chose that specific person for the assignment. God took his time on each us so much that he says, "For *I know* the plans I have for you, plans to *prosper you and not to harm you, plans to give you hope and a future*" (Jeremiah 29:11 NLT). God knows *exactly who* he has called and appointed to fulfill his work on this earth. You lack nothing, there is nothing wrong with you, you are not a failure, *you are not your addiction*, you are not the things people did to you, the things people said to you that hurt you deeply are not true, and God has not forsaken you. You are made *fearfully and wonderfully* in the image of God (Psalm 139:14 NLT).

When God is ready to do something in this earth with the person he calls, he is going to do it whether we are ready or not. One of my favorite stories in the Bible is about Moses and how God called him *knowing his weaknesses*. In the book of Exodus, God calls Moses to go to Egypt and free the people of Israel because they have been enslaved for hundreds of years. God did not ask or look for Moses's input or vote because *he already knew the gifts and the things that he put on the inside of him*. In chapter 4 verse 10 (NLT), Moses, like many of us, began to plead with God. Moses says, "O Lord, I'm not very good with my words. *I never have been*, and I'm not now, even though you have spoken to me."

Like majority of us, Moses began to tell God his problems. He told God why he was not the man for the job and counted himself out all because of his weakness. Not only did he doubt himself, but in that moment, he was also doubting God and the calling over his life. *Have you ever felt like you were about to be free from the addiction or the bondage but then told yourself that you couldn't? Have you ever got a vision that you could be living in purpose but talked yourself out of it because of your past or addictions or flaws? Have you ever felt God pulling on you but still went the other way because you felt unworthy of being in his presence because of the addiction or bondage that you are experiencing?* I can personally tell you that I have done all those things thousands of times. But it does not matter how many times you try to ignore God or choose your way. God will not give up on you nor turn his back on you.

In verse 11, God asks Moses, "Who makes a person's mouth?

Who decides whether people speak or do not speak, hear or do not hear see or do not see? *Is it not I the Lord? Now go! I will be with you* as you speak and I will instruct you in what to say." God is so gracious and patient with us that he will let us plead with him, he will let us try to walk away, but in the end, his purpose is going to come forth. When we plead to God "I'm still addicted to alcohol," "I'm still addicted to pornography," "I'm not qualified for this," "I'm still in bondage," or anything that we may be struggling with, God is aware 100 percent of our struggles. When God called Moses, he wasn't looking at his flaws—*he was looking at the purpose he created him to do.*

If you are reading this, *God is not determining your purpose based on your problems or addictions that you may have.* He is not determining your purpose off your educational background or degrees you have. He is not determining your purpose off your popularity, status, or power. *He is determining your purpose from the fact that before you were ever conceived by your parents that he made plans for you, gave you a purpose, and promised you victory.* You may be struggling right now, but in the end, you will be victorious by the favor and guidance of our all-powerful God. For the rest of this chapter, I want to break down what being devoted to breaking the addiction or bondage means and being devoted to God and your purpose.

The first step to being devoted is to have a *desire.* Desire can be described as simply as turning your heart toward God from the addiction, your feelings or pain. Having a desire starts as a choice or a want for change or purpose. Yes, it is hard to desire when you are in chains of bondage or in addiction. *I know what it feels like to feel as if you can't desire because you're so weighed down from the chains. I know what it feels like to have the enemy get in your head and lie to you and tell you that there's no point because you are too far gone.* Not only me, but also *God wants you to get your desire back.* Once you get your desire back, that's when a relationship with God can form again and actually become even stronger than it was in the past.

You don't have to take this huge step toward wanting to desire freedom or God. All you have to do is put forth effort, and God will handle the rest. In Zechariah 4:11 NLT, it says, "Do not despise small beginnings, *for the Lord rejoices to see work begin.*" God is so good that all he wants to see is you trying. Once you start to begin to have a desire, God, through the Holy Spirit, will begin to work in you and increase your desire for freedom and his will. In Philippians 2:13 NLT, it says, "For God is working in you *the desire and the power to do what pleases him.*" When God begins to work in you, he will turn your desires into his desires, and when your desires turn into his desires, he then gives you the power to do his will. Today I personally want to tell you to choose to have a desire for God. Have a desire for reading your Bible every day. Have a desire for praying when things are good or bad. Have a desire to break the chains that are you holding you back from freedom. Taking this small first step is scary, but it can transform your entire life, push you into freedom and, eventually, into the purpose that God has for you on this earth.

The second step to being devoted is to *eliminate*. Truthfully, the addiction or the bondage that you may be experiencing isn't what you are or what your life is. *It is a distraction to keep you from becoming who you really are.* We must eliminate the distractions out of our lives that are holding us back from really becoming devoted to God and whom he has called us to be. That may be *friends, habits, hobbies, a toxic relationship, or your comfort zone.* It is impossible to obtain all the things that God has for us if we never eliminate the things that are the complete opposite of him. In Hebrews 12:1 NLT, it says, "Let us strip off *every weight that slows us down,* especially the sin that so easily trips us up and let us run with endurance the race that God has set before us."

It does not have to be a sin; it can simply be the people you are hanging out with, the type of music you listen to, your hobbies, or even what you watch on television. Yes, it is hard to let go of the people or things we really want or even the things that we like doing, but if we are going to serve God and live in purpose, we must eliminate. We can't have it both ways or live a double life. In Matthew 16:24 NLT, Jesus says, "If any of you wants to be my follower, *you must give up your own way,* take up your cross and follow me." Either we are going to eliminate the things that are draining us/holding us down or we are going to want to hold on to them all because they bring us comfort. Most of the time we choose the things or even people that keep us bound or stuck because we are comfortable, and we don't want to face anything or experience trials.

At this moment, write this down: THERE IS NO GROWTH IN COMFORT. If we choose to stay in our comfort zone, months or even years will pass us by, and the whole time, we will be going in circles doing the same thing instead of growing and maturing into a purpose-filled life. *God will not do the things that you have the power to do.* There are certain areas in our lives that we cannot pray our way out of. We have to make a conscious choice and actively remove them ourselves and want to make a change, then God will step in and guide us into what he has by his grace. *Anything that we give up for God comes back in a way that we actually need it.* God can't bless us if we never let him be in control of our lives by eliminating the things that don't bring us any value. *He does not share the spotlight.* Today I want you to challenge yourself to eliminate the things that are keeping you bound and to do less while God does more.

The third step to being devoted is to have *vision*. Visualize yourself coming out of this addiction stronger than ever. Visualize the chains being broken off you by our Lord and Savior Jesus Christ. Visualize you being an example of our Father's amazing grace. Visualize yourself being used by God despite your past/scars. Without vision, we cannot have a desire to do the things that God has called us to do. *Where there is vision, there is focus, and where there is focus, there is change or purpose.* If we cannot visualize ourselves winning in the end or living a purpose-filled life, we will never get there. Not literal vision by what our eyes can see, all of us need to have vision and faith for what our eyes *cannot* see no matter the circumstances or how we are feeling. In Hebrews 11:1 NLT, it says, "Faith shows the reality of what we hope for, it is the evidence of things *we cannot see.*" None of us can predict what the future holds or what tomorrow may bring, but all of us can put our hope and faith in Jesus Christ when it comes to beating our addictions/bondage and becoming who we are meant to be.

The fourth step to being devoted, which is the toughest one to do, is *obey*. When God shows you something or tells you to do something or gives you a vision of what your future could look like, *are you going to obey him or tell yourself or him that you can't do it?* When God shows you something or puts it on your heart to do something, it is for a reason. It means that God is trying to do something on this earth *through you*. You may still be struggling with the addiction, sin, or bondage that you're in, but *can you obey him even when things don't look right?* People on this earth who you don't know are depending on your obedience to God. Your purpose and the things that God wants to do through you is not about you. *God wants to use you to get people closer to Jesus, to impact people, and to elevate his kingdom.*

Like we said before, God is not looking at your addiction, weakness, or bondage. He is looking at the gifts he put in you and how everything ties together for your purpose. Stop waiting for the "right time" to start obeying God. Stop waiting to get "cleaned up" so that God can use you. God sent his one and only Son to die for us *while we were still sinners* (Romans 5:8 NLT). He didn't wait for us to get cleaned up to save us; he saved us in the midst of our trouble and hopelessness. *Start that book. Start that small group. Start praying for people. Start the devotionals. Start making those videos. Slow obedience is disobedience.* On the other side of your obedience, there is reward; there is a blessing and breakthrough. On the other side of disobedience, there is disappointment, failure, and heartbreak. In 1 Samuel 15:22 NLT, it says, *"Obedience is better than sacrifice,* and submission is better than offering the fat of rams." God is saying he would rather you obey him and you are in the pit or still in bondage than you being free from the addiction or anything that you're going through and not obey him. All our Father is looking for is for us to obey his commands when he tells us them.

The fifth step to being devoted is to *trust* God. All of us have to trust that God has everything under control. Even when there are things that are outside of our control and we are in a deep pit or still struggling with the addiction, we need to trust that God is a man of his word and that he never breaks promises. Even when it looks you're in a losing season and nothing is going right, keep trusting him. *Even when we don't feel it, God is working. Even when we don't see it, God is working. God never stops working.* God knows the beginning and the end of your life. He is the alpha and the omega; he has been where you're currently struggling at right now. He knows your middle, he knows your struggles, he knows your pain and bondage; he knows exactly where you are right now. In Proverbs 3:5-6 NLT, it says, "Trust in the Lord with all your heart, *do not depend on your own understanding.* Seek his will in all you do and *he will show you which path to take.*" When the things that you are going through do not make sense, when your back is against the wall and there seems to be no way out, or when it seems that you are stuck in bondage, *there is purpose in all those things.* God is so good that he will pave the way for you and give you instruction in your losing season or if you are still struggling with the addiction and bondage. *Depend on God,* not your thoughts, opinions, feelings, or how things look right now.

The sixth step to being devoted is to *expect.* Expect that God is going to blow your mind. Expect that God is about to deliver you from the addiction. Expect that God is about to take your chains and scars and make you an example of his grace. Expect that God can do the unthinkable or the impossible. In 1 Corinthians 2:9 NLT, it says, "No eye has seen, no ear has heard, and *no mind has imagined what God has prepared for those who love him.*" God already has something for you; it is already said and done in heaven, it was done before you were born, it was done before your addiction came, it was done before you ever fell into bondage. The question that you have to ask yourself is, *"Do I really expect God to do things that he promised me?"*

The seventh and last step to being devoted is to be *disciplined.* After you have done all first six steps, this is the most important step that we all have to *maintain.* This process of being devoted *does not get easier; you get stronger.* The first step of you desiring turns into you becoming disciplined. If I am being 100 percent honest with you, there are days when I do not feel like reading my Bible, and there are days when I do not feel like praying. The only thing that keeps me going is my desire for God and to do his will.

Discipline will always follow desire. Being disciplined does not always feel good, it is not always enjoyable, and you're not always going to want to be disciplined, but the reward from being disciplined is better than any reward you can imagine ever getting. In Hebrews 12:11-13 NLT, it says, "No discipline is enjoyable while it is happening, *it is painful!* But afterward there will be a peaceful harvest of right living for those who are trained in this way. So take a new grip with your tired hands and strengthen your weak knees. *Mark out a straight path for your feet so that those who are weak and lame will not fall but become strong."* When you become disciplined, you then become stronger through Christ and will be able to do the things he has called you to do.

I hope and pray that this chapter helps you get started on becoming devoted to not only beating your addiction or bondage, but also to being devoted to following God and seeking his perfect will and purpose for your life.

Prayer: Heavenly Father, today I choose to become devoted to you. I want what you have for me and not the things I want for myself nor the things this world has to offer me. Teach me your ways, show me the things that you desire, and help me desire the same things that you do. Help me eliminate the things that hold me down, help me visualize myself beating my addiction and living in my purpose, give me the confidence and strength to obey the things that you tell me, help grow my trust and faith in you, create in me a new heart so I can expect great things from you because of my obedience, and help me stay disciplined when I feel like giving up or giving in to the things that are keeping me bound. In Jesus name, I pray all these things. Amen.

Chapter Four

TEMPTATION

Even after God delivers us from the addiction that we have been struggling with, temptation is a daily battle for all of us as people of God. As a believer of Jesus Christ, temptation never goes away; if anything, the temptation to give in to our addiction or sin increases because the enemy is creeping and waiting for us to fall back into old habits or addictions. In 1 Peter 5:8 NLT, it says, "Stay alert! Watch out for your great enemy the devil. *He prowls around like a roaring lion looking for someone to devour.*" The enemy's main tactic is to get you to sin so that he can try to disconnect you from God and disrupt your relationship with him and your purpose.

Temptation is anything that promises satisfaction at the cost of obedience to God. No temptation that the enemy tries to throw at us is not going to be anything undesirable or ugly; *they are going to be exactly what we like doing, what we want, or even toxic people and toxic behaviors.* We all need to be aware of our weaknesses and where we are not strong at. It is very important to not think we are stronger than we really are. Truthfully, all of us are weak and cannot beat temptations on our own; we are all human beings, and our nature is to sin because we were born into iniquity or sin (Psalm 51:5 NLT). All of us need the power and the strength of the Holy Spirit, but take heart, everyone on this earth experiences temptations every day, some possibly even the same exact ones that you experience.

In 1 Corinthians 10:12-13 NLT, it says, "*If you think you are standing strong, be careful not to fall.* The temptations in your life are no different from what others experience. *And God is Faithful. He will not allow the temptation to be more than you can stand. When you are tempted, he will show you a way out so that you can endure.*" The reality of it is all of us are going to be tempted, and our Heavenly Father knows that. He is faithful and will never leave you to be tempted or tested by something that you are not aware of nor can handle. But the thing is, instead of giving into the temptation, *pray first*, then God will provide the way out. This may be you going to your Bible to read, playing worship music, going for a walk or run, talking to a trusted friend or family member, or anything to get your mind off what is tempting you. The temptation is not stronger than you nor is it stronger than our Heavenly Father.

There are three truths about temptation that all of us need to know. The first truth is *it's not a sin to be tempted*. When our Lord and Savior Jesus Christ walked the earth, he was tempted just like we are every day. In Matthew 4:1 NLT, it says, "Then Jesus was led by the Holy Spirit into the wilderness *to be tempted by the devil.*" Jesus was tempted by the devil three times in this chapter. The enemy attacked Jesus with temptation when he was at his *most vulnerable* state when he was hungry, he tempted Jesus to try and test God by telling him to throw himself off high ground and that God's angels will catch him, and he tempted Jesus with power and all the kingdoms of the world if he bowed down and worshipped him.

All three of Jesus' responses to the temptations have one thing in common: Jesus said, *"It is written." He fought the temptation of the enemy with the word of God.* Instead of using his own strength, he used the word of God as his weapon when he was most vulnerable. Any temptation that we face, Jesus understands what we are feeling. Yes, Jesus was God, but he was also human; *there is nothing that we experience in this life that he does not understand.* In Hebrews 4:15 AMP, it says, "For we do not have a High Priest who is unable to sympathize *and* understand our weaknesses *and* temptations, but *One who has been tempted [knowing exactly how it feels to be human] in every respect as* we are, yet *without [committing any] sin.*" Temptation is a daily battle that all of us are going to have to face in our journey with God, but Jesus understands what we are going through. We can fight and beat temptation by quoting scripture to ourselves or out loud just like Jesus did and go to our Father in prayer and ask him for strength, guidance, and wisdom for a way out or comfort. *Our Father wants to helps us, but first, it requires us not trying to do things in our own strength and allowing him to do so.*

The second truth about temptation is that *God will never tempt you.* God's intentions are never to tempt us; *God intends to test us for us to be better.* The enemy's intention is to tempt us with evil motives behind them. In James 1:13-15 NLT, it says, "And remember, when you are being tempted, do not say 'God is tempting me.' *God is never tempted to do wrong, and he never tempts anyone else.* Temptation comes from our own desires, which entice us and drag us away. These desires give birth to sinful actions." Anytime a temptation is presented to us, it comes from the enemy because he knows the desires of our sinful nature (or our flesh).

God may put us in a situation or season that may test our faith in him or our relationship with him, but he will never present us with something that has to do with sin for evil intentions. *Temptation is an invitation to depend on Christ.* God may test us or put us in difficult situations because *he wants us to depend on him and only him, not our own strength or what we think is right.* As stated earlier in the chapter, we are too weak to handle things on our own; automatically by nature, we want to sin. It is only through the power of the Holy Spirit that we are able to beat temptation.

The third truth about temptation is that *there is always a way out.* I want to go back to 1 Corinthians 10:13, which says, "*But God is faithful,* who will not allow you to be tempted beyond what you are able, but with the temptation *will also make the way of escape that you may be able to bear it.*" Yes, the testing or the trials that God uses to shape us may be hard and at times they may even feel unbearable, but God is so faithful that even when it seems like your back is against the wall and you can't fight any longer, he provides a way out. *It is only up to us to seek him and ask for wisdom and the perspective for a way of escape.* But what happens when you give in to the temptation instead of taking the way of escape that God provides for you? When we do willfully sin, when we do ignore God, when we fall short of his glory, it is very important that we do not close ourselves off from God and conceal our sins.

In Proverbs 28:13 NLT, it says, "Whoever conceals their sins does not prosper, *but the one who confesses and renounces them finds mercy.*" We need to come clean with God when we do mess up or fall into sin; *God can't bless or help us where or we pretend to be or pretend that everything is okay when they are not.* God will never rebuke you or push you away if you are honest with him about the sins that you commit. In 1 John 1:9 NLT, it says, "*If we confess our sins, He is faithful and just to forgive us of our sins* and to cleanse us from all unrighteousness." God wants to forgive us, he wants to reestablish our relationship with him through forgiveness, and he wants to be a part of our mistakes and our fallings so that he can heal us. Not only is it important to confess your sins to God, but all of us should also confess our sins to trusted people in our lives so that we can be healed fully. In James 5:16 NLT, it says, "Therefore *confess your sins to each other* and pray for each other so that you may be healed."

Healing fully comes from being open and honest about the things that we struggle with and our sin. Prayers from righteous people over your life are powerful and produce healing through the Holy Spirit. It is human to fall into sin and short of the glory of God; that does not make you a bad person or a bad Christian. Every time we fall, God is always there to pick us back up by showing us compassion and extending us grace.

In order to rely on God when faced with temptation, it is very important that we have a close relationship with him. There are three ways that I believe all of us can get close to God and remain close to him. *The first way is talking to God through prayer.* Having a strong prayer life is the backbone of your relationship with God. Imagine yourself with your best friends, girlfriend, boyfriend, or spouse; all of us would agree that communication is a major part of our human relationships, right? It is the same thing with God; since God is not here physically with us anymore, *the only way of communication to the Father is by praying in the Spirit.* In Ephesians 6:18 NLT, it says, "With all prayer and petition *pray [with specific requests]* at all times [on every occasion and in every season] *in the spirit.*"

The most amazing thing about being a child of God is that we have a right and privilege of talking to God about anything at any time; God is always ready to have a conversation with us and listen to us. God hears everything that we pray to him and wants to answer everything that we ask according to his will. In 1 John 5: 14 AMP, it says, "This is the [remarkable degree of] confidence which we have *[as believers are entitled to]* have before Him: *that if we ask anything according to his will,* [that is consistent with His plan and purpose] *he hears us.*" If you do not have a prayer life, I want to personally encourage you to begin to develop one. It was not until my prayer life changed that I really started seeing a change in my habits and me eventually being free from my addictions.

Communication with God is not just a monologue, *but it is actually a dialogue!* God speaks back to us after we seek him and ask him for our requests. Now how can God speak to us if he's not physically here with us? Do we hear an audible voice or see supernatural things? Rarely sometimes yes, but the main the way that God speaks to us is through the Bible. *The second way to get close to God is to meditate on his word.* Every day all of us should set aside time after we pray to read the Bible. The only way to hear or see what God is trying to tell us is to spend time in his word and mediate on it. In Joshua 1:8 AMP, it says, "This Book of the Law shall not depart from your mouth, but *you shall read [and meditate on] it day and night,* so that you may be careful to do [everything] in accordance with all that is written in it; for *then you will make your way prosperous, and then you will be successful.*"

God longs to have a relationship with us and talk to us every day; he wants all of us to live according to his will. But it is up to us to want to make time to hear from him. If you do not read your Bible, I want to encourage you by starting out just reading one verse or one chapter a day, then eventually, your appetite and stamina for his word will grow. I personally started with a verse a day, which then eventually grew over time by doing a little bit each day, which then grew to reading chapters a day. It is important to form a habit of going to God's word after we pray; that is how we will hear God's voice.

The third way to get close to God is through temptation. I know that sounds different and contrary to beating an addiction, but temptation invites us to depend on God. By now, we know that we are too weak to handle temptation on our own because our flesh automatically wants to sin or do what pleases us. God will be strong for us when we are weak; God is our refuge in times of trouble, God is who we should run to when temptation or problems come our way, God is our rock. In Isaiah 26:4 AMP, it says, "Trust [confidently] in the LORD forever *[He is your fortress, your shield, your banner], For the LORD GOD is an everlasting Rock [the Rock of Ages]*." When we put our trust in God and only him, he then can become strong for us. *God cannot be strong for us as long as we are acting strong or as long the thing that we are addicted to is strong for us.* I want to personally tell you to trust God with what it is you are battling with. God will not let you down; he will not shame you, he will not look at you differently, he will not judge you, and he will not abandon you. God wants to help you and be strong for you because you are his child, and he loves you dearly. At this moment, choose to trust God with your addictions or problems. I am praying for you.

Prayer: Heavenly Father, I humbly admit to you that I am too weak to handle the temptations of this life or my addictions by myself. I admit that I can do nothing outside of your presence. Today I choose to trust you with my addictions and to lean on you when I am tempted. I ask that you be strong for me at my weakest moments and redeem and restore me of my losses. In Jesus name, Amen.

Chapter Five

WHAT YOU FEED GROWS,
WHAT YOU STARVE DIES

You have probably heard of the saying, "What you feed grows, and what you starve dies," or you have seen it on social media or possibly even in church. This can practically be applied to or used in a lot of things in life. But I personally think this saying was made for addiction. This saying really helped me beat my addictions and set me free. It was one Sunday when I was at church, and the sermon was about battling temptation, and the pastor who was preaching the word kept saying, "What you feed grows, and what you starve dies."

When I was in my seat, I felt the Holy Spirit convicting me and ministering to my heart. I knew God was talking to me specifically that Sunday. At that time, I was still struggling with my addictions to nicotine and pornography. I wanted to be free; I wanted to quit what was robbing me of my joy, happiness, and purpose. I wanted to be free from bondage; I just didn't know how. I remember, on the way to church, I prayed and said, "Father, I'm in your word, I've been praying, and I've been leaning on you to break free, but at times I give in to my flesh and do the things my flesh wants to do. What else do I need to do to be free of these addictions?" When the pastor kept saying, "What you feed grows, and what you starve dies," I got a fresh revelation, and my prayers were answered. The Lord told me, "Son, I will fight for you, and I will be strong for you, *but you need to do your part and fight back and take action.*"

All of us can depend on God, and yes, God will be God and keep us and strengthen us, but having faith in God and not doing anything does not benefit us; *he will not do what we have the power to do.* In James 2:26 NLT, it says, "So then, as the body without the Spirit is dead, also *faith without actions is dead.*" God will always be there for us, he will always speak to us and help us, but *one thing God will not do is make a choice for us.* God will never force himself on us or make us do anything. God gives all of us free will to do whatever we please, but the question is, will we do what he is teaching/telling us to do, or will we still want to do our own things?

The day that I heard that sermon preached at church, I had to go home and look at myself in the mirror and say, "I am going to starve my addiction and flesh while I feed my spirit." *I had to make a choice to take action while God was strengthening me.* I had to have faith that while I would starve my addiction, God would hold me up in his right hand and guide me through the discomfort of the withdrawal symptoms. Starting out, I thought I was strong all because I went to church, prayed sometimes, and read my Bible sometimes, but I quickly realized that just doing the bare minimum with God was not going to cut it. *I failed time after time after time, and I began to even doubt that I could beat the addiction.* I thought I was defeated and was a failure, but then God spoke to me through the Holy Spirit again. God told me, "*Stop trying to do things outside of me. Involve me in all you do, and remain close to me, and this giant in front of you will fall down and will be beaten.*"

This reminded me of the story of King David when he beat Goliath (the giant). There was no way that David alone could beat and take down Goliath in his own strength. David had to rely on the strength of the Lord to beat Goliath. David knew that he was powerless and weak when it came to this challenge; he knew that the only way to victory was through a relationship with God and the power of the Holy Spirit. In 1 Samuel 17:46 NLT, he says, "This day *the Lord will deliver you into my hands,* and I'll strike you down and cut off your head." The Lord will deliver you from the addiction, and then he will give you the power by grace to come in and finish it.

We are often weak because we are not bonded with that which makes us strong. You are only strong on your own for so long; it is a difference between being a "Christian" and having a live and active relationship, having a bond with God. When we choose to starve our addiction/flesh or anything that may have us bound, it is 100 percent normal to have withdrawals or feel weird at first because your body is craving the things that it is used to doing (a substance, porn, lying, pride, anger, or even emotions). The process of starving your flesh is going to be uncomfortable, it is going to seem impossible, it may even hurt, but through a bond with God, he will keep you strong through this process.

In Ephesians 10:6, it says, *"Be strong in the Lord [draw your strength from Him and be empowered through your union with Him] and in the power* of his [boundless] might." Your strength for beating the addiction or temptation does not come from your own power; the strength comes from God because you are in union with him. Outside of God, it is impossible to do anything or defeat a giant that is in front of you. All of us need the power of the Holy Spirit dwelling inside of us to do anything in this life.

Now that we've talked about starving our addictions and flesh, what about feeding our spirit? I believe there are three ways that we can all feed our spirit when the desires of our flesh are dying. *The first way to feed your spirit is with prayer.* As we talked about in chapter four, prayer is simply having a conversation with God. When you are starving the desires of your flesh, it's as if you are dying to yourself because you are denying the temptations of your own desires. When you are starving your flesh, the devil is going to attack you with all types of temptations, urges, feelings, thoughts, or even flashbacks of the thing that you are addicted to. The only way to fight off his evil schemes is through praying to our Heavenly Father.

Not only is prayer talking to God, *but prayer also strengthens your spirit.* In Matthew 26:41 NLT, Jesus says, "Watch and pray so that you will not fall into temptation. *The spirit is willing but the flesh is weak.*" Have you ever been tempted by something and you know in your heart that you don't want to do it? You know it is wrong and that there are consequences for your actions, but you do them anyway? I personally know that feeling all too well, and I have been where you are currently at if you are struggling from breaking free.

A lot of us choose to do what the enemy is tempting us to do because *our flesh is weaker than our spirit. Through prayer is where we get the strength in our spirit to fight off the temptations or urges of our flesh.* All of us want to do the right thing, but unless we involve God and rely on him through prayer, we will always follow our own desires, which creates bondage, which then leads to us becoming far from God. If you have fell into your own desires 1,000 times, you can always get up 1,001 times and lean on God; he will never give up on you or turn his back on you. If you sin, fail, or fall short of his glory 1,000 times, he will forgive you 100,000 times. There is not an exact number of how many times God will forgive you; *his forgiveness and love for you is infinite because you are his child.*

The second way, I believe, that we can feed our spirit is with the word of God. When all else fails, we can always turn to and rely on God's word. In Isaiah 40:8 NLT, it says, "The grass withers, the flowers fades. *But the word of God stands forever.*" No matter what you are going through, no matter how many times the devil lies to you and tempts you, no matter how many times you fail, no matter how many times you fail to receive God's forgiveness and grace that he offers, no matter how messed up you think you are, *the word of God stands for eternity and never changes.* The word of God is the playbook for living a life as a Christian. It is the blueprint of how we are to walk every day as children of God. The more we read his word, the more we become like him. The more we read his word, the more we begin to see a change in our mind and our perspective. The more we read his word, the more we begin to trust him and the promises that he tells us.

The most important part about reading the Bible *is to actually live by the things that you read*. In Psalms 119:9-11 NLT, King David says, "How can a person stay on the path of purity? *By living according to your word*. I seek you with all my heart; do not let me stray from your commands. *I have hidden your word in my heart that I might not sin against you*." Imagine taking a class when you were in high school or college. The teacher can lecture you, give you study tips, tell you exactly what chapters to read in your text book, or even have a test review. But until you actually apply the things that they teach or tell you for the upcoming test or quiz, you would fail every time.

It is the same thing in life and with God. *God will always speak to us and give us a fresh revelation while we are reading the Bible, but the question is, will we apply it into our life?* Will you actively live according to what you are reading even if it makes you lose people, even if it is uncomfortable, even if it makes you look crazy? I want to be honest with you if are reading this—*there will be no change in your life or your habits until you start applying and actively living out God's word*.

The amazing thing about the word of God is that when you are actively reading it every day and start applying it to your life, *it begins to saturate your heart*. A sign of true spiritual growth and maturity is when you get to the point where the word of God is so embedded in your heart that you don't even want to sin anymore. It is when you don't want to give in to the enemy or your own desires and everything you want to do will be to honor the Lord. It is when the enemy throws all types of lies and schemes at you and you refuse them because scripture is hidden in your heart. Today I want to challenge you to escape your comfort zone and start reading the Bible and applying it to your everyday life. Yes, you may lose people, people may insult you, you may even feel lonely or weird. But the opinions of others and your feelings do not matter when it comes to living for God. He sees you stepping out on faith and living according to his will; he sees how it makes you feel. *When you start moving in faith because of his word, God will then begin to move in your life*.

The third way, I believe, that we can feed our spirit is being with the right people. I can testify and personally tell you that *you turn into the people you put yourself around.* When I first became addicted to the things that I struggled with and now battle with, it all started from me being around the wrong group of people. No, the people who got me started with my addictions are not bad people; they just weren't the right people for my destiny, life, or purpose. Think about it this way: Imagine a glass of water and one drop of a toxic chemical is dropped into the water. Now the entire glass is contaminated and filled with toxins.

It is the same with your life; *it honestly only takes one person to toxify your life and your habits.* This can be with your friends, coworkers, or even family. It is impossible to become who God created you to be if you have bad company in your life. You can be doing everything right and spending time with God, going to church and even serving, but if there is a hint of toxicity in your life, you'll slowly start to become like the people you are hanging out with. In 1 Corinthians 15:33-34 NLT, Paul says, "Do not be misled: *Bad company corrupts good character.* Come back to your senses as you ought and stop sinning." In the process of you starving your addictions/flesh, *if the enemy cannot get you to sin through tempting you in your mind, he will use the people around you who are already stuck in sin.*

It is very important that you surround yourself with people who are good for you and your purpose even if that means you only having one to two friends; there is nothing wrong with that. I would rather you have one to two friends who mean you good and have good intentions and actually care and love you than for you to have ten or more friends who are really snakes in the grass and mean you evil or harm. *At this moment, write down the name of all the people who are currently in your life, and ask yourself, "Are they adding value to me, or are they taking value from me?"* If they are not adding value to you, I want to encourage you to let them go; it is not personal, but if you want to see change or freedom, you must let go of the people who are not helping you. *It is okay to be alone, it is okay to feel alone; with God, you are never alone.*

God is so good and loves you so much that if you fail to remove the people who does not add value to your life, he will, which does hurt, but it's not meant to hurt you; *it's meant to separate you.* Sometimes God will do the things you won't do so that he can get you moving. Letting go of people we care about or the people who have been in our life for years is scary, and it is hard, but God can't do what he's trying to do as long as the wrong people are still present in our lives.

At this moment, I want you to write down one of the three ways that will help you feed your spirit or one that you could focus more on. Maybe you do have a strong prayer life, but you don't really know God's word. Maybe you know God's word, but you can do better with having a prayer life. Maybe you do pray, and you do know God's word, but the people you are currently hanging around aren't good for your life. Choosing one of the three will help you grow in a specific area, which will then roll over to all three areas. I am praying for you, and I hope you begin to feed your spirit more than your flesh.

Prayer: Heavenly Father, today, at this moment, I willingly choose to starve my addictions/flesh and feed my spirit. I ask you that forgive me for feeding my selfish desires and not feeding my spirit or my relationship with you. I repent from the things that have had me bound, and I turn toward your everlasting love. As I feed my spirit with prayer, your word, and righteous people, I ask that you create in me new desires and a new want to live off the things you tell me and not the things of this world. In Jesus name, Amen.

Chapter Six

LIVING BY THE SPIRIT

In the past two chapters, we have talked about temptation—what it is, how to battle it, and how to feed your spirit while you are starving your own desires. But now that we've done all those things, how are we supposed to live? Can we just go back to how we were doing things before? Do we sometimes rely on God, only when we're in trouble? Do we live a lukewarm Christian life? *After we have beaten temptation and starved our desires, it is important that we live by the Spirit.*

When we begin to live and walk by the Spirit, we begin to act like God, see like God, respond to things like God, and our desires turn into his desires. In the process of beating the addiction that you may struggle with, walking by the Spirit eliminates the desires of your flesh and actually enhances what your spirit wants. In Galatians 5:16-17 NLT, Paul says, "So I say, *walk by the spirit. And you will not gratify the desires of the flesh. For the flesh desires what is contrary to the spirit and the spirit what is contrary to the flesh. They are in conflict with each other so that you are not to do whatever you want.*"

Every day God wakes all of us up, there is always a conflict between our flesh and our spirit. The flesh will always want to do the opposite of what your spirit wants and vice versa. For example, if someone makes you mad or does something to you that you don't like, your flesh wants to cuss them out, hit them, or do the same thing they did to you back to them. Your spirit wants to forgive them, love them, and help them with their heart issues. When someone asks you for money or a favor, our flesh does not want to give or help the person who is in need. Your spirit wants to give to them, serve them, and show them love the way Jesus shows us love when we call on him for help. It is the same way with your addictions/desires. *Your flesh wants the thing that you have been habitually doing for weeks, months, or even years. Your spirit wants you to quit, be free, and live by the spirit in close union with God.* But how do we overcome the appetites of the flesh and live by the Spirit? I believe there are two ways that all of us can walk freely in the Spirit that God graciously gives to us.

The first way to overcome the appetites of the flesh is to *depend on the power of the Holy Spirit.* As we have talked about in the past two chapters, it is impossible to beat or do anything if we do not have God or the power of the Holy Spirit. Yes, temptation is a very real thing; urges may begin to become unbearable, and our desires make us feel good. But truth be told, we are not obligated to our desires or the temptation that the devil may throw at us. In Romans 8:12-13 NLT, Paul says, *"You have no obligation to do what your sinful nature urges you to do. For if you live by its dictates, you will die. But if through the power of the Spirit you put to death the deeds of your sinful nature, you will live."*

The same Spirit that rose Jesus Christ from the dead is alive and dwelling inside of us—simple fact that all of us should rest and have confidence in. If you are a child of God, you have the Holy Spirit literally dwelling inside you, giving you the strength to do anything in this world. There is nothing on this earth that is stronger than the Holy Spirit, even the devil himself. *You are above addiction, you are above temptation, and you are above sin.* All of us have the authority over the enemy and his evil schemes; he may lie to us, he may try to deceive us, but he is not stronger than us. In Luke 10:19 AMP, Jesus says, "I have given you authority [that you now possess] to tread on serpents and scorpions, *and [the ability to exercise authority] over all the power of the enemy (Satan)*; and nothing will [in any way] harm you." Write this down in your notes or even highlight it: THE ENEMY HAS NO POWER OVER ME.

The enemy only has one play when he tempts you to sin. All he does is show you the good side of temptation/sin; he will never show you the consequences that sin has when you commit it. *Sin thrills, then it kills.* Sin has the power to kill your joy, happiness, peace, self-control, confidence, self-esteem, and most importantly your relationship with God. Like we talked about earlier in chapter two, it's not that your addiction or sin will push God away from you, but your addiction/sin will push you away from God because of the shame and condemnation that the enemy throws at you when you do slip and fall. We must stand strong and rely on the power of the Holy Spirit that is alive in us. *"He who is in you is greater than he (Satan) who is in the world [of sinful mankind] (1 John 4:4: AMP)."*

At this moment, write this down in your notes or put it somewhere you can see it every day: I ADMIT THAT I AM POWERLESS OVER _____. I BELIEVE THAT THE POWER OF GOD WILL HEAL ME AND MAKE ME WHOLE. It is important that you are honest here with what it is you are fighting so you know what to fully give God and depend on him for. *What remains covered will not be healed.*

The second way to overcome the appetites of the flesh is to *follow the prompting of the Holy Spirit.* As children of God, the Holy Spirit prompts us to do things every day. For example, the Holy Spirit may prompt you to give to the people who can't pay you back or buy someone lunch when you are out at a restaurant or love the people who have hurt you or just simply being nice to others. The Holy Spirit is who guides our steps and our paths as children of God. To put it simply, the Holy Spirit is our GPS. He will give us turn-by-turn instructions on what to do, what to say, and how to handle certain situations we face in this life.

It is the same thing when it comes to beating addiction and temptation; all of us must pay attention and follow the Holy Spirit when he prompts us. When we are tempted to indulge in what it is we like doing, the Holy Spirit is actually prompting us the second we are tempted. That is why you begin to contemplate, "Maybe I shouldn't do this," or "I want to do it, but I know afterward I'm going to feel bad," or "I know it's bad, but God is going to forgive me, so I might as well just do it, right?" These are all tactics and tricks that not only the enemy uses on us, but they are tricks that our mind and our flesh tells us also. In Galatians 5:24-25 NLT, it says, "Those who belong to Christ Jesus have *crucified the flesh with its passions and desires. Since we live by the Spirit, let us keep in step with the Spirit.*" Yes, your feelings and your wants are very real, but when it comes to living by the Spirit and moving by the Spirit, they are a bad indicator to follow. Your feelings and your flesh will lie to you, make you do things you wouldn't normally do, indulge in things you know is bad, not only for your health, but also for your spirit, because by nature, we want to satisfy ourselves.

Starting today, when you are tempted or when you feel an urge to indulge in the thing that you are addicted to, I want you to not move so quick to do it. When you are tempted, *slow down and take note of every time you sense the Holy Spirit prompting you.* Here are ways that you can know when the Holy Spirit is beginning to prompt you: *when you feel like something you're about to do is wrong, when you feel off about something, when you have a gut feeling that the choice you're about to make is going to harm you or others around you, when you feel a conviction, when you feel remorse after doing it, when the choice you did make is stuck in your mind and you feel like you need to pray.* When you begin to feel these promptings, it's not that God is mad at you or he's in heaven saying, "If you do this again, I'm not forgiving you this time." *The fact that you feel him prompting you through the Holy Spirit shows that you truly are a child of his.*

Think of it this way, any good parent is going to prompt or talk to their child before they make a bad choice or a mistake. Our human mother or father is going to tell us, "Darrian (or your name), you shouldn't do that," "I don't feel comfortable with you doing that," "Be careful," or "I don't really like the group of people you have been hanging out with lately." It is the same thing with God; the only difference is he is not here physically, so he goes deeper and connects with us through the spiritual realm and our conscious. In Romans 8:16 AMP, the apostle Paul says, "The Spirit himself *testifies and confirms together with our spirit [assuring us] that we [believers] are children of God*." Count it all joy when the Holy Spirit prompts you; this means that you and God are in tune and he is speaking to you!

I hope and pray that this chapter helped you and pushed you to live life led by the Holy Spirit. I want to encourage you to listen to what our Father is trying to tell you in the midst of the temptations/urges that you may experience. I am praying for you.

Prayer: Heavenly Father, today I choose to live my life by the Spirit. I ask that you give me the discernment to know when it is you prompting me. I ask that I as I decrease, you increase and that the Holy Spirit gives me the courage and the power to live a life that pleases you. I admit that I cannot live the way that I want to and see change. Forgive me for trying to do things my way. I choose you and your way. In Jesus name, Amen.

Chapter Seven

THE VOICE OF GOD VERSUS THE
VOICE OF THE ENEMY

As children of God, we hear two voices in our life while we are here on earth: the voice of God and the voice of the enemy. I believe that it is very important that we have the discernment to notice which of the two we are hearing because if we are not careful, it is easy to get deceived by the enemy and fall into sin, bondage, and temptation. Now how do we hear the voice of God or the enemy? Are they audible voices? Is it a whisper? Sometimes rarely, yes, but most of the time the voices that we hear come to our minds. Jesus talks to us on a regular everyday basis, but the conflict that we have with that is a lot of the times the outer world and sometimes the enemy is louder than the voice of God. Our spiritual enemy named the devil and his demons roam the earth, distracting the people of God, wanting to pull us away from our Father's presence, voice, and purpose for our life.

In Revelation 12:9 NLT, it says, "And the great dragon was thrown down, the age-old serpent who is called the devil and Satan, *he who continually deceives and seduces the entire inhabited world*; he was thrown down to the earth and his angels were thrown down with him." The enemy distracts us many ways by using things like social media, the opinions of others, our addictions, and our problems and throws lies at us and tries to condemn and shame us. *The nature of the enemy is to lie; the nature of God is truth. The nature of the enemy is evil; the nature of God is goodness and love. The enemy's voice will always contradict God's voice; everything he says to you or shows you is the exact opposite of what God says or sees in you.* For example, the enemy may call you an addict, but God calls you a daughter/son. The enemy may tell you that God can't use you because you are too far gone, but God says he wants to use your past, your mess, and your current situation to bless others and elevate his kingdom. *The enemy calls you by your sin, but God calls you by name.* I believe there are six principles that can help us discern the difference between God's voice and the enemy's voice.

The first way to discern if it is God or the enemy is *God's voice will convict you but in love; whereas, the enemy's voice will bring guilt and condemnation.* God is a God whose nature is always to love because God is love (1 John 4:8: NLT). God will never condemn you or convict you with bad or evil intentions or because he is mad at you. He convicts you because you are his child and he loves you. Like we talked about in the previous chapter, any good parent is going to prompt their child to do better or want to lead them into better things if they are heading down the wrong road.

When God is convicting you by the Holy Spirit, he is not punishing you or mad at you; he is doing it because he loves you beyond comprehension and doesn't want you to fall into something that is going to harm you even more, like anxiety or depression, which could turn into suicidal thoughts or attempts. God convicts you of something because he wants you to come back to him and to remain in his presence, even if you have messed up or sinned. In 2 Corinthians 7:9 AMP, the apostle Paul says, "Yet I am glad now, not because you were hurt and made sorry, *but because your sorrow led to repentance [and you turned back to God]; for you felt a grief such as God meant you to feel, so that you might not suffer loss in anything on our account.*" Until you come back to God and repent, he is always going to convict you because he does not want you outside of his presence. He will use the Holy Spirit, he will use people in your life, he will use anything this world to get you back in his presence because he loves you that much. He will even leave the ninety-nine just to come after you and get you back.

The enemy is the exact opposite. When we do fall or mess up or sin, he wants to keep us there in our mistakes. He wants to put us in a place of bondage where there is no more communication with God, a dark place, and may even begin to tell us that God would never forgive us. He begins lying to us and whispers in our ear, "Look at what you did," "This is all your fault," "You're not good enough for God to use," "When people find out what you go through, nobody will love you or look at you the same," "You might as well just give up now." I personally have struggled with this, and if I am being honest, there are times when I believed the lies of the enemy and stayed in a place of bondage. If you are experiencing this and feel like no one understands, I understand you, and I relate 100 percent to you.

As I stated earlier in this book, there is nothing wrong with you, you are not too far gone for God to love or use; you are not a failure, you are not your addiction, you are not what the enemy or anyone else calls you. You are a child of God who is called and set apart for our Father to use. There is no shame nor condemnation for you because you are a child of God and in Christ. Rest in that fact today.

The second way to discern if it is God or the enemy is *God's voice will encourage and reassure; whereas, the enemy's voice will discourage and frighten.* God wants you to be free from the addiction or the bondage that has you in chains. God will encourage you and reassure you that everything is going to be okay, even if you are in the middle of a storm. *God reassures us who we are and who he is when we are struggling with our addiction, and he encourages us to keep fighting, even if it seems like we're never going to overcome it.*

The enemy is going to discourage you or even frighten you from beating your addiction and becoming who God has ordained for you to be. He will tell you things like "How can you help other people when you have problems of your own?" "Maybe you should wait and get cleaned up first," "Nobody in your family has ever done something like this. What makes you different from them?" "Don't forget what happened last time when you tried stepping out on faith and trusting God." When you begin to hear or think these thoughts, they are nothing but the enemy trying to attack you. Don't let the enemy win by lying to you. You are victorious in all that you do because you have Jesus!

The third way to discern if it is God or the enemy is *God's voice will lead, guide, and keep you still; the enemy will push and rush.* When battling addiction or bondage, God will lead you even while you are in the pit and there seems to be no way out. In Psalms 23:3 AMP, David says, "He refreshes and restores my soul (life); *He leads me in the paths of righteousness for His name's sake.*" God loves each and every one of us so much that he is willing to meet us where we are at and lead us by his way and his righteousness. God will literally change you inside and out when you allow him to lead you. If you are still struggling with pornography, pills, alcohol, anxious thoughts, self-esteem issues, or anything that has you bound, that does not scare God away from you. He wants you to come to him as you are, and he will begin to speak to you and lead you down the path that he has for your life, *for his name's sake.*

Think of it this way: The messier you think you are, the more people talk about you, the more people even reject you, *the more glory God gets out of it in the end.* God is willing to lead you because he wants to make you an example and witness of his love and his grace. When people say "He/She is too far gone," "It doesn't surprise me that he/she relapsed into the addiction," "They have a lust problem, they're never going to find love," even when you begin to doubt yourself or maybe even doubt God, I strongly believe that God is in Heaven saying, "Oh, this just makes the testimony better," "He/She is the perfect person I want to use in the world for my glory." As we talked about in chapter two, God's ways are not our ways, and his thoughts are not our thoughts. Today I want to encourage you to let go of the opinions of others or toxic thoughts that you keep telling yourself and let God lead you as you are.

Not only will the voice of God lead you, but his voice will also guide you. It does not matter where you are with your walk with God; he will never stop guiding you, *even in the darkness.* In Psalms 23:4 AMP, David says, *"Even though I walk through the [sunless] valley of the shadow of death,* I fear no evil, *for You are with me;* Your rod [to protect] and Your staff [to guide], they comfort and console me." If you are in a pit right now, struggling with your addiction or you're in bondage, God is guiding you right now as we speak. *It is no coincidence that you are reading this book; it is not by mistake. God is currently guiding you by the Holy Spirit to remain close to him and to trust him, even when things do not look right.*

Imagine you and your family/friends are going on a road trip, and you end up taking the wrong turn. Now you are in the middle of nowhere, and its starting to get dark outside with you barely having any service on your phone, and it is on 10 percent battery. As you keep driving, you begin to realize that there are no more streetlights, street signs, or even other cars around you. Most of us, including myself, would begin to feel a little nervous and on edge. The only way to get to your destination is to go to your maps and type in the address of the place in your phone. You now have to trust that Siri knows the turn-by-turn directions to guide you on where you are trying to go, and you have to follow it. It is the same thing with God; you may have made the wrong turn in your life by bad choices or the people you've been hanging out with, you may have relapsed into the addiction that you once beat or may be struggling with anxious thoughts again, and now it seems like you are in a dark place. The only way to get back on your feet and to experience deliverance is to put your trust in God and his guidance for your life. Today, at this moment, I want you to make the choice to trust the guidance of God's voice and what he is telling you; he will not abandon you nor leave you out to dry.

Third, the voice of God will keep you still. When we begin to overthink, put thoughts that are not true in our mind, or begin to have anxious thoughts, God's voice will bring you stillness and give you peace. I love the story when Jesus and his disciples were going to Gadarenes, but on the way there, they ran into a storm. The most fascinating thing about this story is that Jesus was on the bottom of the boat sleeping. He was with them, and his disciples knew Jesus personally, and they trusted him, but as soon a trial came, they began to panic. When the disciples saw the storm, they freaked out and began calling on Jesus for him to save them. When Jesus woke up, he told them, "Why are you afraid, you men of little faith?" (Matthew 8:26 NLT). *After he told them that, he immediately rebuked the winds and the sea, and there was a great calm.*

This reminds me of how we are and how we react when things in life do not go our way. When we fall back into sin, or we relapse, or we lose people we love, we begin to panic and begin to freak out, calling upon the Lord. The most amazing thing about this story is that Jesus asked them, "Why are you afraid?" God wants us to trust him and fear nothing that is in this world, no matter what comes our way or how many failures we have. *God will always still your storms or your anxious thoughts if you let him, but instead of us staying there, it is important that we accept his stillness and move on, not looking back at our failures.* If we look back at our past or our failures, that is where mental bondage comes in, and that will leave a doorway for the enemy to come and try to keep us bound.

It is also important for us to recognize and acknowledge who God is and when he stills us. When we run into problems or trials, it is human nature to try and take them head on and try to fight them in our own power or our way. Honestly, if we had the power to beat our addictions, bondage, or temptations on our own, we would have been victorious. God will take you through a season of giants and allow affliction in your life that you cannot beat outside of his presence because God wants to be acknowledged and depended on. In Psalms 46:10 AMP, God says, *"Be still and know (recognize, understand) that I am God. I will be exalted among the nations! I will be exalted in the earth." God wants us to know and recognize that he is the only one who has the power to really keep us still and comfort us;* not a substance, not other people in our life, not the things we watch, not things we listen to, not a hobby, or not even our favorite pastor.

In the midst of trials, if you ever feel compelled or in a rush to do something that pleases you for a temporary moment, that is the enemy. The enemy will always push or rush you into something that is not God. The enemy knows what we are addicted to or our struggles, so he will always try to throw your desires at you as an alternative for God. Today I want to challenge you to replace the thing that gives you pleasure with God, going to him in prayer. No, you're not going to get the buzz or the high that your flesh craves, but your spirit will experience the peace from God, which transcends all human understanding (Philippians 4:7 NLT), and that is better than anything that is in this world.

The fourth way to discern if it is God or the enemy is *God's voice will calm us; the enemy's voice will make us obsess and worry.* The voice of our Father is a calming, loving voice, which does not bring any worry. Many times throughout the Bible you see God calming storms or situations that had his followers (disciples) scared. I want to return to the story of the disciples and Jesus when they were in the middle of the sea.

I want you to think about this: If Jesus can sleep peacefully in a thunder storm in the bottom of a boat, possibly getting rocked back and forth and soaking wet, why should we fear or worry about anything that this life has to throw our way if Jesus is with us in our boat? It isn't that Jesus was not aware of the storm that him and his disciples were going through; Jesus had faith that they were going to get through the storm together to their destination where God was sending them to. *The winds and the waters did not wake Jesus up; the cry out/voices of his followers woke him up.* That is when he got up and calmed the storm and told his disciples, "Why are you afraid, you men of little faith?"

Don't you find this amazing? Complete chaos can be going on in our lives, but Jesus remains calm until he hears us cry out for him. He then speaks to us and calms us and reminds us that everything is going to be okay as long as he is involved. All we have to do is whisper, and he will hear us. Jesus hears the tear running down your cheek at two in the morning, when you can't sleep; he hears and sees the pain that you are going through because of your addiction/bondage, he sees you struggling to beat the giant that is in your life. It is in those moments when he does the same exact thing that he did with his disciples in the boat; he calms us by talking to us. Jesus will never have you worry or have you fear that he will not come through for you in the moment of need.

The enemy is the complete opposite of what Jesus does. In the middle of our storms, the enemy wants us to obsess and worry about the things that we are going through. He will begin to put thoughts in your head like "When will this ever stop?" "Am I really ever going to get better?" "Does God really still love me after all I have done?" "Why do I keep relapsing or doing the things that I do not want to do?" *Today I want you to read and mediate on Philippians 4:6 (NLT), then put it somewhere where you can see it every day.* This verse has helped me so much in my life and, honestly, got me to where I am currently at. It says, *"Don't worry about anything; instead, pray about everything.* Tell God what you need, and thank him for all he has done." The key to beating any anxious thoughts or worries is through prayer to God. God wants to hear from you and carry all your burdens while you carry his, which is easy and light. Today I want to encourage you, if you are anxious or worried about your future, your purpose, or your life, to go to God in prayer with an open heart. I promise, our Father is eagerly waiting to hear from you.

The fifth way to discern if it is God or the enemy is *God's voice will bring comfort; the enemy's voice will bring chaos and compromise.* The voice of God will always comfort us in hard and uncomfortable times. If you are still struggling with addiction, God is there comforting you. If you are still in mental bondage, God is there comforting you. If you are currently hurting, God is there in the midst of your pain comforting you. In the middle of your withdrawals or cravings, God is there to comfort you with those feelings. *God never has and never will take his hand off your life, no matter how bad things get.* Imagine that you have kids, and they are hurting or struggling with something. As a parent, all of us would want to be there and comfort our child to best of our abilities. We would show them unconditional love, be there to talk to them, be an example for them, and want to comfort them, right?

It is the same exact thing with God, except his comfort and love goes much deeper than we could ever imagine. In Isaiah 66:13 NLT, God says, *"I will comfort you as a mother comforts her child."* No matter where you are in your life at this moment, God is comforting you. It breaks God's heart to see his children go through things that hurt and drain them spiritually. Today go to God as you are, even if you are still addicted or in bondage, and let the voice of God, through prayer and his word, comfort you.

Not only does God comfort you in the middle of your trouble, but he also prepares you and gets you ready so that he can use you when it is time to help comfort your coworkers, friends, or family. In 2 Corinthians 1:3-4 NLT, it says, "Blessed be the God and Father of our Lord Jesus Christ, *the Father of mercies and the God of all comfort, who comforts and encourages us in every trouble so that we will be able to comfort and encourage those who are in any kind of trouble, with the comfort with which we ourselves are comforted by God."* Like we talked about in chapter two, there are certain things that you are currently going through right now that looks like it is over or that it is impossible to beat or that you are too far gone. God is currently preparing you for something that is much bigger than the current struggle that you are in or even yourself. As I look back over my life, the exact things that I struggled with are the exact areas where God wants to use me. I had to go through the fire in order to turn into who God has called me to be. *If you are reading this, the same thing goes for you! You are currently on your way to what God has for you if you endure this season and keep walking with him, even in your mess.*

The enemy is the exact opposite in an evil way. When you begin to feel cravings or withdrawals from the thing that you are addicted to, he will begin to bring chaos to you mentally and have you compromise your obedience to God for a temporary feeling. He'll starting pushing you, and you will start thinking things like "you know you want to," "nobody has to know," "nobody is going to find out, it's not that big of a deal," "you might as well do it since you have the access to it." He did this same exact thing with Adam and Eve in the beginning of time. In Genesis 3:1 NLT), the devil says,

"*Did God really say* you must not eat the fruit from any of the trees in the garden?" He made Eve question what God told her; he twisted the word of God and deceived Eve, and she gave into the temptation that compromised her obedience.

Maybe the enemy tells you things like "Did God really say that he would comfort you?" "Do you really believe that God will never leave nor forsake you, even though you keep messing up?" "Do you think waiting on God is going to feel better than you having a drink or smoking this?" The enemy will always have you compromise your obedience and relationship with God for the temporary pleasure your flesh desires.

The sixth and final way to discern if it is God or the enemy is *God's voice will bring Christ closer; the enemy's voice brings controlling spirits.* For anything that he tells you, God will always point you to Jesus in every possible way. It is through Jesus and only Jesus that you are connected to God, so God will always want to bring Christ closer to you in anything that is going on in your life. The day when you believed and accepted Jesus Christ as your personal Lord and Savior, the Holy Spirit pierced your heart, and now Jesus lives within you. In Ephesians 3:17 NLT, the apostle Paul says, *"Then Christ will make his home in your hearts as you trust in him. Your roots will grow down into God's love and keep you strong."* The fact that Jesus lives within you shows that when God speaks to you, it will always point back to Jesus; it does not matter if you are still addicted, still in bondage, still struggling with temptation or deep in a pit. *He chose you and loved you long before you chose him.* Once you accept Jesus in your heart, he will never leave.

The voice of the enemy brings controlling spirits which have the power to control your mood or even the things you do. Things that are controlling spirits in this world that affect you can be *anxiety, depression, stress, fear, doubt, uncertainty, addiction, bondage, and temptation.* Like we talked about a few chapters ago, the devil can't hurt you physically, so he will throw things at you that are mental and things you can't see coming. The only way to fight these controlling spirits is with God and having a personal relationship with him. Without God, it impossible to beat these spirits in our own strength.

I hope that this chapter gave you insight and better discernment on the difference between the voice of God versus the voice of the enemy. I pray that you continue to seek God and allow his voice to be bigger than the enemy's and the things that are in this world. I am praying for you.

Prayer: Heavenly Father, I ask that you continue to speak to me in ways that I know. I ask that you grant me the wisdom to know when it is you speaking to me and when it is the enemy lying to me. I submit to your voice, and I choose to follow your voice and your instructions instead of my own understanding and own choices. In Jesus name, Amen.

Chapter Eight

THE FIGHT WE DON'T SEE

When it comes to us battling our addictions, anxiety, depression, or any type of bondage that is in our life, there is a real fight that happens in the spiritual realm that our eyes cannot physically see. *This is what we call spiritual warfare.* Anything that we experience here on the earth is nothing compared to what really goes on in the spiritual realm. In Ephesians 6:12 TPT, the apostle Paul says, *"Your hand-to-hand combat is not with human beings, but with the highest principalities and authorities operating in rebellion under the heavenly realms. For they are a powerful class of demon-gods and evil spirits that hold this dark world bondage."* I know this verse is a lot to take in, so let's break it down together.

The main thing I want you to realize is that we live in a very sinful, fallen, and evil world. In previous chapters, we have talked about the devil and his demons that currently roam the earth. I want to return to that verse (Revelation 12:9 NLT), and I want to explain the back story so you get a full understanding of how our enemy works. In this piece of scripture, it says, "The great dragon, the ancient serpent called the devil, or Satan or the one deceiving the whole world— *was thrown down to the earth with all his angels.*" Before the devil and all his angels (demons) were cast out of heaven, there was a spiritual war happening in the heavenly realm with God's angels and his demons, which resulted into them being thrown out of heaven onto the earth.

A little back story about the devil—once upon a time, he was God's favorite angel. When he was in Heaven, he was in charge of the music, he was attractive, and he was very smart. At some time that we don't know of, the devil became proud and wanted to become higher than God in Heaven with his angels (now demons). So as a result, the devil started a war in Heaven, which caused him to literally fall to the earth like lightning. Why am I telling you a story about the devil? Because he is the reason that sin exists today. In the book of Genesis, he shows up in the garden of Eden to tempt Eve in the form of a serpent. In Genesis 3:1 NLT, it says, "The serpent was the shrewdest of all the wild animals the Lord God had made. One day he asked the woman, Did God really say you must not eat the fruit from any of the trees in the garden?" And as you know, Eve ended up being deceived and ended up falling into temptation, which resulted in the entire world being cursed with sin.

Just like he tempted Eve with deception, he does the same exact thing with us every day. He whispers in our ears lies that are not true, shows us things that we know we are attracted to that will cause us to stumble, attacks us in our most vulnerable states, and twists God's word. Also, his demons come in many forms, not the exorcisms, body twisting, foaming at the mouth kind. Yes, those are real, but that rarely happens. Majority of demons that come after us are depression, anxiety, lust, anger, pride, greed, and addictions of any kind. Like we talked about in the chapters of temptation, the devil will never tempt you with something that he knows you are not attracted to or things you do not like doing. He will always tempt you with something that you like.

Our enemy and his demons are attractive things in the physical world but, in the spiritual world, are 100 percent evil and mean nothing but harm to our lives. It is so important that we recognize when spiritual attacks/spiritual warfare is occurring in our personal lives. I believe there are seven signs of spiritual warfare that we can all look out for as signs that spiritual warfare has begun in our lives. These signs are *changes for the worse (health, finances, relationships), temptation to sin beyond the normal, patterns of recurring negative thoughts, severe discouragement, crippling condemnation, intimidation and fear, and confusion.* I want to break each of these seven things down so you can get a full understanding of what we are talking about.

When we begin to feel sick, lose our job, or other traumatic events, it may or may not be a spiritual attack, but at the same time, it very well could be an attack from the enemy. A lot of times that is just life, and unfortunate circumstances always happen. But if you begin to always feel like you are losing things, sick, or experiencing traumatizing events, this could definitely be a spiritual attack. The enemy always comes to steal, kill, and destroy, so he is always looking for ways to disrupt our lives, put us in a position of pain, and have us doubt/question God and why he would allow this to happen. When things happen to us in the physical world, it first has to pass through God. Satan literally has to get permission from God to do things to you. *Today rest knowing that if you are sick, have lost a job, or are experiencing or have experienced traumatizing events, God is well aware of it, and he is faithful enough to restore you of everything.*

Like we have been talking about for the majority of this book, all of us are going to want to sin automatically because that is our nature as human beings. The temptations that we face originate from our own weakness and ungodly desires, but the enemy can use situations and people around us to apply extreme or sudden pressure on us in these areas. When you begin to feel sudden pressure to sin, do the things that you struggle with, or do something that you don't normally do by your atmosphere or people, this is very well a spiritual attack. Our enemy knows that he can't have us if we are in Christ, so what he does is use stressful or overwhelming situations or even people around us to get us to fall into sin, which can drag us away from God and have us become lost sheep. *I want to encourage you to be watchful of the environments and people you put yourself around; they can be the catalyst for you falling into sin or back into old habits.*

When we begin to start having negative thoughts constantly going through our mind, this is definitely a spiritual attack as well. When you find yourself beginning to question God, doubt that he is real, or your faith wavering, that is a spiritual attack on your mind. Like we talked about in the previous paragraph, if you are in Christ, the enemy cannot have you. There is nothing in this world that he can do to get you, so one of the main things he does is attack the minds of God's children. If you are having negative thoughts go through your head all day and even at night, I want to encourage you to pray to our Father and ask him for his peace, which transcends our human understanding. Yes, you may be hearing things in your head, but the thoughts themselves are not real; that is the enemy or one of his demons whispering lies in your ear. *Do not listen to these thoughts; listen to the word of God, and trust what he says in the Bible.*

It is 100 percent human to feel discouraged at times. All of us go through discouragement if it has to do with a goal, with what God has called us to do or something that God put on our hearts to do. But when we the discouragement is so heavy to the point where you're scared, that is a definite spiritual attack. Like we talked about in chapter two, the enemy knows how powerful we really are and that if we were to ever fully step into the things that God has called us to do, we could make hell tremble. I want to personally tell you, if God has called you to do a certain thing or fulfill a certain purpose on this earth, there is not a demon in hell that can stop that nor the devil himself. He can discourage you and tell you things all he wants, but if you begin to move and eventually fulfill what God is trying to do through you, it will come to pass. *Rest today knowing that no amount of discouragement can take your purpose away from you.*

As we have talked about in previous chapters, there is no shame or condemnation for anyone who is in Christ. The Holy Spirit convicts us, but our enemy condemns us. Conviction is out of love and guidance, while condemnation is evil and has bad intentions. If you are feeling condemned for your past or even your present mistakes, this is another sign of a spiritual attack. The enemy always will want to put us into shame or condemn us because that is what will hold us back from coming to God for peace, guidance, stillness, wisdom, or forgiveness. The enemy knows if he can get us to believe that shame is enough to keep us from God, we will never be healed, forgiven, or reach our purpose. Our Lord and Savior Jesus Christ took all our shame and condemnation two thousand years ago on the cross. Every feeling of shame about your past or present was nailed to the cross with Jesus. *If you are battling with shame or are feeling condemned, today rest knowing that if you are in Christ, there is no shame for you. Whether it be from past mistakes/sins or present struggles, you are set free by Jesus.*

When you begin to feel intimidated or scared that is nothing but the enemy attacking you. God does not give us these emotions/feelings; as a matter of fact, he gives us the exact opposite of those. In 2 Timothy 1:7 AMP, it says, "For God did not give us a spirit of timidity or cowardice or fear, *but [He has given us a spirit] of power and love and of sound judgement and personal discipline [abilities that result in a calm, well-balanced mind and self-control].*" The enemy's goal is to always scare us, have us stuck in fear so we won't move into things, or even make us fear God in a negative way. When we begin to truly realize that fear will never come from God, fear will never have its reign over us again. If fear ever creeps in your mind or begins to affect how you walk and move with God, this is a definite spiritual attack on your mind. If you have been struggling with fear and it is affecting your everyday life, I want to encourage you to take it and lay at the feet of the Lord and trade burdens with him.

Have you ever been confused to the point where you don't even know what to do or how to move? This is another spiritual attack from the enemy. The enemy thrives in confusion; we think it's us, and everything begins to get hazy. Confusion is often an attack on our minds and is meant to keep us stuck so we won't progress with what God is trying to do in us and through us. Just like fear, God does not give us confusion. In 1 Corinthians 14:33 NLT, the apostle Paul says, *"For God is the God of harmony."* When you begin to feel confused about something, rest knowing that it is not God who is making you feel that way; it is the devil. If you have been confused or stuck because you do not know what is next, I want to encourage you seek God and ask him for guidance, wisdom, and discernment.

So how do we fight off these spiritual attacks? How are we supposed to fight something that we can't even see? Because we are in battles that we cannot physically see, we all need to fight less in the physical realm and more in the spiritual realm. In Ephesians 6:13 TPT, it says, *"Because of this, you must wear all the armor that God provides so you're protected as you confront the slanderer, for you are destined for all things and will rise victorious."* The only way to win a fight that we are too weak for is to use the things that God gave us. I want to talk about the six strategies that Paul says in verses 14-19 we can use to fight spiritual attacks every day.

Strategy no. 1: Truth. In verse 14, Paul says, "Put on truth as a belt to strengthen you to stand in triumph." When we truly realize the difference between truth and lies, we will truly be set free from the bondage that comes from us struggling. Yes, you may have an addiction that you battle with, you may have a weakness that only you and God know about, you may find it hard to believe that you are accepted and loved by God, you may think you're too imperfect for God to use, or you may not see yourself the way God sees you. But the truth is you are not the addiction that you battle with. You may have a weakness, but that does not disqualify you from the purpose that God has ordained and spoken over your life. You are 100 percent accepted and loved by God because of your faith in who Jesus is and what he did on the cross. You are not too imperfect or too far gone for God to use according to his purposes in this earth. You are fearfully and wonderfully made in the image of God and capable of doing every work that he put inside of you. When we know the truth, we will always win spiritual attacks that come from the enemy. And who is the truth? The truth is Jesus. In John 14:6 NLT, Jesus says, *"I am the Way, I am the Truth, I am the Life.* No one can come to the Father except through me." When we realize that Jesus is the truth and he is the only way to God, especially through spiritual attacks, we need not to fear anything the enemy throws at us or tries doing to us. If you do not know Jesus, I want to encourage you to stop reading and open your heart and accept him. Pray out loud, "Jesus, I believe that you are real, that you came, and that you died just for me. I want a relationship with you, and I want to know you. In your name, Amen."

Strategy no. 2: Holiness. In verse 14, Paul continues on to say, "Put on holiness as the protective armor that covers your heart." I want all of us to realize that God is holy and the enemy is the exact opposite. In a spiritual attack, the enemy wants you to do things that are not holy so he can get you separated from God. When the enemy is attacking you, always ask yourself, "Would this be considered holy? Would God want me to do this?" The more you lean on holiness, the less room there is for the enemy to attack you. The more you resist him, the more he will flee from you. I want to encourage you today to lean more on holiness and who God is than what the circumstances look like or the feelings that you are currently experiencing.

Strategy no. 3: Faith. In verse 16, Paul says, "In every battle, take faith as your wrap-around shield, for it is able to extinguish the blazing arrows coming at you from the Evil one!" Faith is putting our hope in God and the things that he promised us that we cannot physically see. Faith is the evidence of things that we cannot physically see, and it is impossible to please God without faith. When the enemy is attacking you, if you're in a season of loss/struggle, if you are still wrestling with your addiction or still feeling bound by your past, it is vital that we keep our faith in the darkness. As long as we have faith in whose we are and who God is, we will always come out of our struggle. If you are wavering in your faith, I want to encourage you to pray and ask God to strengthen your faith and trust in him. That does not make you weak, and he will not push you away for asking him for strength. God is always here to help us, but he will never kick down our door to help us.

Strategy no. 4: Salvation. In verse 18, Paul says, "Embrace the power of salvation's full deliverance, like a helmet to protect your thoughts from lies." If you have accepted Jesus Christ as your personal Lord and Savior and are saved, the devil knows that he cannot have your soul. So what he does is attack your mind and lies to you about everything. He will twist scripture, call you your struggle, accuse of you of not being good enough for God, will tell you that you are too far gone, that you are not worthy to be loved by God, that you can't do something because of your habits, and will threaten you with condemnation. When we fully embrace what Jesus did for us on the cross, the enemy is defeated. As a matter of fact, the moment you accepted Jesus into your heart, he was defeated. The enemy cannot take away your salvation nor can he disqualify for what God has called you to do. Today rest in the fact that there is nothing the devil can do to take away your salvation or the Holy Spirit from you.

Strategy no. 5: The word of God. In verse 18, Paul continues on and says, "And take the might razor-sharp Spirit-sword of the spoken word of God." Using the word of God in a spiritual attack is the most powerful and important strategy we can use on beating the enemy. Us being in spiritual warfare without using the word of God is like showing up to war and not having any bullets. When all else fails, the word of God will forever stand strong and be our strongest weapon. Remember when we talked about the enemy attacking Jesus when he was in the wilderness? Jesus was in one of his most vulnerable states because he was weak from starvation and being in a literal desert for forty days and nights. He used the word of God as his defense against the lies and schemes of the enemy. If you are struggling with spiritual attacks from the enemy and don't know what to do, you can always turn to and rely on the true written word of God.

Strategy no. 6: Prayer. In verses 18-20 Paul says, "Pray passionately in the Spirit, as you constantly intercede with every form of prayer at all times. Pray the blessings of God upon all his believers. And pray also that God's revelation would be released through me every time I preach the wonderful mystery of the hope-filled gospel. Yes, pray that I may preach the wonderful news of God's kingdom with bold freedom at every opportunity. Even though I am chained as a prisoner, I am his ambassador." I know that this was a lot, so I want us to break it down together. As we talked about in the previous chapters, prayer is simply having a conversation with God. Pretty much, prayer is a dialogue; as we pray up to Heaven, God will speak back to us if it is through his word or through the day-to-day things we do. When the enemy is attacking you, what better way to involve God in the attacks than to talk to him? God is never burdened or annoyed at the amount of times that you pray. The enemy wants you to think that you can't go to God because you keep praying the same thing over and over. That is a lie from the pit of hell. God always wants us to talk to him and to hear from us. If you have to pray eighty times in one hour because the attack is so strong, then so be it! God would rather you pray to him all day than go through everyday life and not talk to him at all.

Not only should we be praying for ourselves when we are experiencing spiritual warfare, but we should also be praying for every believer in this world. Why? Because all of us who believe in Jesus Christ and his resurrection are a family in him. No, we are not family by blood, but we are family through Jesus Christ. Every believer in the world is experiencing some type of spiritual warfare, attack, or temptation of some sort. When we realize that us being born again is not just about us, but about God, his kingdom and his children, the more souls and people will begin to get saved and redeemed, the more we can rise up as a family against the evil one, the more we can elevate the kingdom of God. If you do not pray for the people around you, you know or even those you don't know, I want to encourage you to begin to pray for others. The most powerful thing that any of us can do is pray. Never underestimate the power of your prayers; your prayer matters, your prayer changes things, your power shifts things, you prayers can shift an entire atmosphere. The more we pray, the more power God can give his people. How can God move or help us when we never talk to him or just simply ask him? Today I want to encourage you to begin to talk to God; he is longing to hear from you, and he is eagerly waiting to talk back to you.

In verse 20, Paul says, "Yes, pray that I may preach the wonderful news of God's kingdom with bold freedom at every opportunity. Even though I am chained as a prisoner, I am his ambassador." I want to return to what we talked about in chapter two. I have the same question that I asked you in the first chapter: *What are you chained to?* I want all of us to realize, no matter the situation that we are facing, no matter the battles that we are currently in, no matter the amount of pressure that we feel, no matter how much the enemy tries to make us fall, God has an assignment for our lives that is already predestined to happen. Paul is saying that he will preach the wonderful news or the word of God with bold freedom at every opportunity he has. Not only that, but he also says that statement while being in literal chains in a prison. Paul is an excellent example to follow when we are experiencing trials, pressure, or even in chains of our own lives. My question for all of us is, can we still operate in purpose while being chained to something? Can we still have the want or desire to serve God even if things aren't going our way? Can we still choose God even if our current circumstances don't look like what he promised us? All of us should strive to be like Paul and choose that no matter how things look or how we feel, we are going to serve God and spread the gospel. If you are still battling with the chains you have, I want to encourage you to first ask God who you are in him, then begin to move by faith. As you move by faith, the chains that seem heavy will begin to fall off you, and God will use your chains for his glory.

I pray that this chapter helped you learn what spiritual warfare is, the signs of it, and the different strategies that we can use to fight it off and beat it. I am praying for you.

Prayer: Heavenly, as I begin to experience spiritual warfare, help me realize that I am not fighting against myself or other people. Help me lean on you and trust you when the enemy is attacking me. I need your strength and the Holy Spirit to help me conquer the enemy. Help me to always seek you first and to use truth, holiness, faith, salvation, your word, and prayer to fight off the attacks of the enemy. I can't do this alone. In Jesus name, Amen.

Chapter Nine

ASHES TO BEAUTY

Have you ever seen a picture of a mosaic? If you haven't, pause on reading, get your cell phone or laptop, and go to Google and search what a mosaic is. Pretty amazing and beautiful pictures, right? A mosaic is a picture that an artist creates out of broken glass, stone, or even sand. The artist takes literally every single broken piece and transforms it into a beautiful masterpiece, which then goes on display in front of other people. This picture is the exact example of what our Heavenly Father does with all his children.

We serve a God who specializes in taking things or people that are broken, lost, rejected, betrayed, shamed, or hurt and turns them into beautiful masterpieces. He takes everything that we have been through, every bad choice, every failure, every addiction, every season of anxiety or depression and uses those things to make a beautiful masterpiece that he uses for his glory. He will rise all of us up from the ashes that we may experience in this life. In Isaiah 61:3 NLT, it says, *"He will give a crown of beauty for ashes,* a joyous blessing instead of mourning, festive praise instead of despair. In their righteousness, they will be like great oaks that the Lord has planted for own glory."

There is nothing that you have been through or are currently going through that God cannot turn around for you. I speak hope and restoration over your life today; this is not the end of your story. As a matter of fact, this is just the beginning. If you are reading this, the Lord is eagerly wanting to take you from ashes to beauty. He just wants you to trust that he is the only one who can do so. It may feel like God has left you in the ashes or in a dry season, but God is there in the ashes with you. He's currently sitting there with you in the ashes as we speak, giving you peace. I want to talk about one of my favorite people and stories in the Bible, the story of Job.

The book of Job is about a righteous man of God who honored the Lord in everything that he did. In the eyes of the Lord, Job never did anything wrong. He always put God first in all areas of his life, whether it be his family, his servants, or his livestock. He was a blameless man and an individual who had complete integrity. He would often even purify his children if he felt that what they did dishonored the Lord in their hearts. He was also the richest person in that entire area and had plenty of land and livestock. We would all agree that Job probably wouldn't ever have to experience any challenges or hardships, right? Like what possibly could wrong, and why would they go wrong if he was a blameless man and honored God in everything that he did? In the first two chapters, God tests Job two times that would ultimately break him.

In the Bible, it says that in heaven, there was a meeting with God and his angels, but then something surprising happens. Our spiritual enemy, the devil, shows up and begins to converse with God, talking about Job. In chapter 1 verse 8 (NLT), *God asks Satan, "Have you noticed my servant Job? He is the finest man in all the earth. He is blameless. a man of complete integrity. He fears God and stays away from evil." Then in the next verse Satan replies "Yes, but Job has good reason to fear God. You have always put a wall of protection around him and his home and his property. You have made him prosper in everything he does. Look how rich he is! But reach out and take away everything he has, and he will surely curse you to your face!" Then*

God replies "Alright you may test him. Do whatever you want with everything he possesses, but don't harm him physically."

In the next few verses, you see Job lose literally everything he has. He lost all his animals, farmhands, shepherds; his servants died, and his children died. Job reacted like all us would react when we lose things that we love. In verse 20, it says, "Job stood up and tore his robe in grief." But next, he does something that majority of us do not do when we are faced with trials in life. In verse 21, it says, *"He fell to the ground to worship the Lord* and he said The Lord gave me what I had and the Lord has taken it away. *Praise the name of the Lord!"* In everything that happened, Job did not sin by blaming God. Job literally praised the Lord in spite of losing everything he has ever had, including his children. *Will you still praise God and thank him for all he does even when things in life go left? Can you praise him in the midst of you still being addicted? Can you praise him in the middle of your mental bondage?* All of us should always praise God, even when we are in the lows of life, not just when things are good. He is always worthy of the praise.

In the next chapter, there was another meeting in Heaven, and yes, you guessed right— Satan showed up once again, and God and the devil were conversing again. God asks Satan the same question he asked him in the previous chapter *("Have you noticed my servant Job? He is the finest man in all the earth. He is blameless. a man of complete integrity. He fears God and stays away from evil even though you urged me to harm without cause")*. But then Satan pretty much tells God that the testing that Job was experiencing was too easy and that anyone could handle that. In verse 4, Satan says, *"Skin for skin! A man will give up everything he has to save his life. But reach out and take away his health, and he will surely curse you to your face!"* God then replies to Satan and says *"All right do with him as you please. But spare his life."* So later on in the chapter, Satan strikes Job, and he is now covered with boils on his skin, from head to toe. Things got so bad that even his wife told him that he should curse God and die, but Job maintained his integrity.

Put yourself in the shoes of Job. How would you handle losing everything you once had in the blink of an eye? Your health takes a major decline, and now your significant other is telling you to curse

God and die. I don't know about you, but me being 100 percent honest, my faith, at this moment, would have wavered, and I don't know what I would have done or how I would have handled it. Job is our prime example of how to endure and persevere in seasons of testing that God allows in our lives. Little did Job know God was intentionally allowing the devil to test him in literally every area of his life because God had intentions to bless Job double-fold with things, people, resources, etc. *God planned to use what the enemy meant for evil for Job's good all along.*

Now wait a minute, if God is allowing the devil to test Job and take everything away from him, doesn't that mean that God is aware of everything that is happening in his life? *The answer is yes!* God was not surprised by the grief and the pain that Job was experiencing. He was not shocked that Job was upset. He was not thrown off by Job saying some of the things he said based on his feelings or emotions. God was 100 percent aware of everything happening in Job's life and had everything under his control.

Now how does this relate to you? God is not surprised at the things that you are currently going through right now. *He knew before he even formed you in your mother's womb that you were going to have a weakness to pornography. He knew that you would have a weakness to a substance that you are addicted to. He knew that you would struggle with anxiety, depression, or even low self-esteem. If you have once quit what you are addicted to but then relapsed, guess what? God is not surprised about that either.* It does not matter how you got to the ashes, what you did to be in a place of ashes, what people did to you that resulted in you being in ashes. God has every intention to bring you out of the ashes and into beauty just like he did Job. He wants to bless you double-fold, he wants to restore your brokenness, he wants to redeem all the time that you may have lost, he wants to open new doors for you, he wants you to beat the addiction that you're struggling in with his help; he wants to prosper you and not harm you.

I want to take a break from talking about this story. *Do you notice the difference between how God and Satan described Job?* God had so much faith in Job that he was willing to let the devil test him, take everything away from him, and even harm him physically. He literally even asked the devil, "Have you noticed by servant Job"? God had faith in a human being that no matter what was thrown his way, he was going to beat it and remain faithful to him during the storms.

I am honestly amazed at the faith that God had in Job. So if God had that much faith in Job, why wouldn't he have the same amount of faith in us? There's nothing different or special about Job; he was not a better human being than we are or had a higher ranking in Heaven than we do. God does not have favorites. God had faith in Job because Job was a child of God. If you are a child of God, it does not matter what has happened, what is currently happening, and what will happen in the future; God loves you and has so much faith in you to the point where he is willing to tell the devil to test you because he knows the ending that both the devil and even ourselves don't know.

If you are in a season of testing, relapses, failures, setbacks, denial, or things not going your way, now is not the time to sin by blaming God or doubting that he exists and loves you. This is the time when you go into your secret place to pray to the Father and dive into his word every day. It is okay to be in the presence of the Lord in grief, hurt, broken, lost, or in tears because he is the only person who can truly repair you and transform everything that is happening into a beautiful masterpiece. That is exactly what Job did, and I personally have had to be in his presence broken and lost plenty of times. That does not make you weak; it makes you human and makes you realize that you truly do need God in your life.

I want to return to the story of Job in chapter 2, where he has now been struck with boils on his body from head to toe. In verse 8, it says, "Job scraped his skin with a piece of broken pottery *as he sat among the ashes.*" Job literally looked around him and at what was going on and just sat there in the midst of everything and waited on God. My question to you is, are you willing to sit in a season where things do not look right and wait on God? Are you willing to let God give you contentment with where you are currently at even if you don't like it and that there is nothing more nor less that you can do to improve things? Are you willing to sit in God's presence broken and hurting so that he take you through a process of healing? Are you willing to walk through a season with God, not ever finding out why something happened? Sometimes it takes more faith to stay in something uncertain than leave something just to be comfortable.

Do you know what the most interesting thing that stands out to me about this book is? God never told Job why things happened the way that they happened. God does not owe us an explanation as to why certain events go on in our lives. God wants us to trust no matter what or how things look or pan out. In Proverbs 3:5 NLT, it says, *"Trust in the Lord with all your heart do not depend on your own understanding."* The more we sit in our feelings trying to figure things out, the more time it is that we are wasting that we could be using for prayer, reading our Bible, or doing the last thing that God instructed us to do.

By trying to figure out everything or trying to make things make sense is giving the devil exactly what he wants. He wants to distract us with worry or curiosity instead of us just trusting God and walking with him. All that is doing is causing more stress and adding on more weight that you can't carry into the next season that God is trying to bring you into. It does not matter how you started the thing that God instructed you to do; it is how you end up and who it ends up blessing or freeing is what really matters.

Today not only me but also God wants you to get your hope back; hope that God can bring you out of this situation, hope that God can turn your ashes to beauty, hope that God still has plans to prosper and not harm you, hope that you can beat the addiction, hope that you can beat the anxious thoughts that go through your mind all day. You know, one of the enemy's tactics is to get you stop hoping. Why is that? Because if he can take away your hope, he has now taken the gasoline away for what drives faith. As we have talked about in previous chapters, faith is the reality of what we *hope* for. If you do not have any more hope for anything, it is impossible to have faith. Then when you don't have any more faith, it is now impossible to please God because we know that it impossible to please God without faith.

Today I personally want to tell you to choose to not believe the lies that the enemy is putting in your head.

I want to return to the story of Job. After he literally scrapes off the dead skin and sits in his ashes (or his current condition) for the remaining of his season, Job's friends came and tried to comfort him. I want to take a detour for just a second; when things in life happen, when disappointment happens, when a storm that you weren't expecting hits your life out of nowhere, when you are going through anxiety or depression, when the addiction that you beat comes back and you relapse, it is so important to have people in your life who will just sit with you and hear you out. Sometimes, if you are a friend to someone you know is hurting and is suffering, it is better to not say anything and just simply be there for them in comfort.

For the remaining of the chapters of this book, except the final five, Job is pleading his innocence to his friends. He tells them in almost every chapter that he did nothing wrong and he does not deserve to be where he is currently at. He began to question God, doubt that God was really with him, and he even cursed the day that he was born and said that he wished he would've died in his mother's womb than be alive in that moment. *Does that sound familiar to you? Have you been questioning God or even begin to doubt if God was real? Have you asked yourself, "If God is so good, why am I going through the things I'm going through?" Have you been having very vivid and dark thoughts about your life? Have you been contemplating suicide or thinking about what life would be like if you were never born or if you were to die?* Not only Job, but I also can relate to you wholeheartedly if you are experiencing these feelings/thoughts. Those thoughts only come from the enemy; those thoughts are not your thoughts. When you begin to hear those voices, that is the enemy or one of his demons lying to you.

Like we have been talking about this entire book, you are a child of God. No matter what you think, no matter what goes through your head, no matter how bad your anxiety gets, no matter how deep the depression gets, the day/moment that you believed Jesus is the Son of God and that he lived and died on the cross for your sins, you were saved and were brought in to God's adopted family of believers. And there is absolutely nothing that you can do that that will take away your salvation. We will talk about that more later on in this book.

After all these chapters of Job talking about God and his life in a negative way, God finally responds and speaks to Job. *Isn't it amazing that even when Job was suffering and was doubting God, God stayed faithful and remained in Job's life and listened to him?* When God spoke to Job, the first thing he did was question Job, like Job has been questioning him. In chapter 38 verse 2 (NLT), God asks Job, "Who is this that questions my wisdom with such ignorant words?" He then begins to ask Job questions that God and only God could answer. In chapters 38-42, God asks Job questions, such as "Where were you when I laid the foundations of the Earth?" "Have you ever commanded the morning to appear and caused the dawn to rise in the east?" "Who created a channel for the torrents of rain?" "Who gives intuition to the heart and instinct to the mind?" After asking Job these questions, God asks Job a question that blew my mind away. God asks Job, "Do you still want to argue with the Almighty? You are God's critic, but do you have the answer?"

I want to return to what we talked about earlier in this chapter. As human beings, we cannot grasp or understand even the slightest thing that God does or his ways. We can try to analyze and break down what happened. We can try and look at the current situation that we are in and try to figure out where we went wrong or why God is allowing affliction or suffering in our lives. But every time we question or even doubt God, we get no answers. The fact is that all of us mere are humans who shouldn't even be doing those things.

In Romans 11:33-36 NLT, the apostle Paul says, "Oh, how great are God's riches and wisdom and knowledge! *How impossible it is for us to understand his decisions and his ways! For who can know the Lord's thoughts? Who knows enough to give him advice? And who has given him so much that he needs to pay it back?* For everything comes from him and exists by his power and is intended for his glory!" *The less we try to figure out what God is doing or why things are happening the way they are happening, the more peace and trust we have that God truly can take us from a place of ashes to a place a beauty.*

Brother or sister, stop trying to figure out where you went wrong, stop replaying in your mind what you did, stop regretting the people you put yourself around, stop feeling shame from the thing you tried once and now you're addicted to. Today I personally want you to choose to not live in shame anymore. No, you cannot take back anything you did or change what was done to you, but you can change what you do at this moment and tomorrow. God wants to take you from your ashes to the beauty of his promises, but he cannot do so if you continue to hold on to and live in your shame and be condemned.

At the end of the book of Job, you see God not only blesses Job, but he blesses him double-fold. In chapter 42 verse 12 (NLT), it says, *"So the Lord blessed Job in the second half of his life even more than in the beginning."* The struggle that you are experiencing right now, the loneliness, the pain, the depression, the anxiety is a set up for God to get the glory out of your life. God's plan all along was to bless Job double-fold when he allowed the devil to test him. Today rest in the fact that whatever you are going through right now, God is going to turn your ashes into glory and is going to bless you double-fold and restore you if you remain in close communion with him. *I prophesy and speak that over your life, but the question is, will you receive that by faith?* I hope this chapter gave you hope and confidence that God is with you and that he is not finished with you. I am praying for you.

Prayer: Heavenly Father, I pray for and I ask forgiveness for blaming you or not thinking that you have been with me through it all. God, I pray that you turn my struggle, my ashes that seem like there is no way out, into beauty. I ask that you give me a hunger and a thirst for your word and increase my devotion and passion to seek you every day through prayer and your word. I ask, God, that as I begin to know you and follow you, that you help keep me patient as I wait on your response and your redemption. I trust you with my ashes, and I trust you with my life. In Jesus name, Amen.

Chapter Ten

REPENTANCE

Repentance, what does it really mean? We hear this word in church, different pastors say it when they preach, and we see it often when we are studying our Bible, but what does it really mean to repent? *The word "repent" in the Bible simply means to turn. When we go to God in prayer and we repent our sins, it means that we are turning away from our sins, our ways, our desires, things that are not of God and all the things that we have done, and we are putting our eyes, focus, and hearts on God.* In the New Testament (all four gospels), John the Baptist was always preaching, *"Repent of your sins and turn to God for the Kingdom of God is near."* Through our repentance, we are acknowledging what we have done or are currently doing is wrong and are reestablishing our connection with God.

Repenting is not just acknowledging that we are wrong or that we have sinned so we just turn to God because we feel bad. True repentance is when we are really sorry for what we have done or what we're currently doing and mean it from our hearts and want to change our ways. I can personally tell you in my own life, when I repented from my

73

bad choices and the things that I was doing, I would always fall back into the same sin over and over. Why? Because I repented just when I felt bad for what I did, I didn't have a true repentant heart. When we are praying to God and we repent, *God looks at our hearts (1 Samuel 16:7: NLT)* and can tell if we truly mean what we are saying. I did not see true change from my repentance until I went into God's presence humbly and meant every word that I was saying to him. I love the quote that Pastor H. A. Ironside said many years ago; it says, *"To repent is to change one's attitude toward self, toward sin, towards God and towards Christ."* When we repent, we're not just changing what we do or our habits; we are changing our attitudes as well.

But how are we supposed to just change our attitude all of a sudden? How are we supposed to just instantly flip a switch in our minds that changes us into a completely new person over night? The answer is we don't. Change through repentance is not an overnight process; *it is a daily process that we all have to want to make in our hearts and let the Spirit do his work within us. It is not about perfection; it is about progression.* In Ephesians 4:23 NLT, it says, *"Let the spirit renew your thoughts and attitudes."* The only way to become more like Jesus is to allow the Holy Spirit to change you from the inside out after you have turned to him. As humans, none of us have the power to just instantly change whenever we want to; our flesh will always be contrary to what the Spirit wants as we talked about in the previous chapters. Our mind and our thoughts have such a powerful role in how we are as individuals, in the things we do and in the things we say.

In Romans 12:2 NLT, the apostle Paul says, "Don't copy the behavior and customs of this world, *but let God transform you into a new person by changing the way you think.* Then you will learn to know God's will for you, which is good and pleasing and perfect." When we repent, we are setting everything we do, even our mind, on God. Imagine yourself breaking a bone in your body caused by an injury. The only way to get the bone that is broken in your body set and put back in the right place is by going to the doctor or a specialist and have them do the procedure. It may hurt; nine times out of 10, it won't feel good, and it may even make you cry. But after the bone is set in the right place and covered by the cast, it can then begin the healing process, which can take up to several weeks, and then it actually turns out to be stronger than it was before.

It is the same thing with God when we come to him in repentance. When we come to him broken, hurt, ashamed, embarrassed, or regretful of the things we have done, *God specializes in taking people or things that are broken and messed up and can heal/ transform them into a beautiful masterpiece.* It might not feel good or right in the moment; there may be a time or even seasons that God prunes away the things that hinders you from being in alignment in his will. Whether it be addiction, habits, friends, or even family, it is inevitable that God does prune us. You may have to lose people and let go of things that you enjoy doing. You may have to spend some time alone in the wilderness with only God so he can work out the problems that are in your life.

But after the pruning season, and you have been made right by God and put in the right environment, you begin to heal and see true change in your life. In the healing process, he will place you around the right people, lead you to a church that best fits you, expose the gifts that he put inside of you, and will cover you with his love, mercy, and grace. As time goes on, you'll begin to experience change and transformation that you would have never imagined yourself experiencing, and you'll end up being stronger than you've ever been. To this day, I am amazed with what God has done in my life by transforming me the way he wanted to, and it all started with me coming to him with a true repentant heart. I want to encourage you today to go to God's presence with a repentant heart; turn to him and let him transform you the way he wants to.

As stated in previous chapters, you are called by God to fulfill his works in this world. You do not have to be perfect to be used by God; as a matter of fact, Jesus did not die for perfect people. Jesus died for imperfect people who do sin so that they can have a relationship with God and so that he can use their imperfections and mistakes for his glory; those people are us. All we have to do is recognize that fact and repent our wrongdoings so that God can do what he has planned before we were even born. In Luke 5:32 NLT, Jesus says, "I have come to call not those who think they are righteous, *but those who know they are sinners and need to repent.*" This verse in itself shows us that we are all sinners, but through us believing in Jesus and repenting our sins, we can walk in purpose without having any doubts. Everything that you have ever done is washed away by the blood of Jesus, and you are now hidden in Christ. In Colossians 3:3 NLT, it says, *"For you died to this life and your real life is hidden with Christ in God. And when Christ, who is your life is revealed to the whole world, you will share in all his glory."*

So not only do we become hidden with Christ and get to live a purpose-filled life, but also all of us get to share his glory on the day that he comes back. I don't know about you, but these verses give me life and fill me up with joy that my past is my past and my mistakes that I make today do not define me as a person tomorrow. *You are not your past, and you are not the things you have done or what people have done to you. You are a joint heir with Christ who has authority and purpose as long you are alive and breathing.*

So what happens when you repent wholeheartedly and went to God with a true intention to change but you still give in to the thing that you know is wrong? When you were younger, you have probably heard your parents, schoolteachers, or any adult figure in your life, say, *"Every decision that you make, whether good or bad, has consequences."* As we talked about in earlier chapters, God has given us the power to make our own choices in our lives, but the question is, what will we do with our free will? *Are we going to accept God's forgiveness, grace, and mercy and live his way, or are we going to rebel and turn our back on God to do our own thing or fill our own desires?*

I remember when I was five years old, and for some odd reason, I was always interested in touching stove tops, whether they were on or off. Both my parents and my grandparents would always tell me, "Darrian, be careful and stop touching stove tops, even if they appear to be turned off and harmless. It may appear to seem like it is not hot, but if you keep touching it, you are going to get burned." They even provided security around the stoves and would cover the stove tops to make sure I wouldn't get burned. But sure enough, one night after we ate dinner, I was curious, and I disobeyed them. I went and touched the stove top because it wasn't on and seemed harmless. Just like they warned me, I got burned by the stove top, and my entire hand had blisters on it. Because I disobeyed them, the consequence that I received was a very serious burn that lasted for weeks to a month.

When I got burned and yelled in pain, my grandparents immediately ran into the kitchen to see what was wrong. When they saw that I disobeyed them, they were upset with me because I was being hardheaded, but they still cared for me and helped me fix what I had done. My grandparents put aloe vera on the burn and hugged me tightly and comforted me instead of yelling at me or chastising me. They actually did not punish me; they wanted to make sure I was okay and that I finally learned my lesson and to obey them when they protect me from something or when they tell me not to do something. They had mercy on the fact that I did not do what they told me to do because they wanted to fix what was causing me pain. Ever since that night, I always have remembered to not touch any hot surface because of what happened and the pain that it brought me.

I know I just told you a funny life story about myself, but I want to relate that back to God and his word and how it all relates to repentance. In Psalms 78, the writer of this book talks about this group of descendants (the warriors of Ephraim) and how they rebelled and turned their backs on God, *even after God had delivered them from their distress and provided for them. They then ended up not doing what God said to do.* In verses 11-18 (NLT), it says, *"They forgot what he had done,* the great wonders he had shown them, the miracles of their ancestors on the plain of Zoan in the land of Egypt. For he divided the sea and led them through, making the water stand like walls! In the daytime he led them by a cloud, and all night by a pillar of fire. He split open rocks in the wilderness to give them water, as from a gushing spring. He made streams pour from the rock making the waters flow down like a river! Yet they kept on sinning against him, rebelling against the Most High in the desert. *They stubbornly tested God in their hearts demanding the foods they craved.*"

At this moment, I want you to pause on reading and look back over your life and recognize or try to remember when God has been beyond good to you, even when you didn't deserve it. God has protected you from things that you have no idea about. The fact that you are reading this right now and are alive and breathing just shows that God has been walking with you and protecting you since the day you were born. *Not only has he been protecting you, but he has also been providing for you.* The school that you are currently attending, the job that you currently work at, and the current people in your life who have your best interest are just a few ways that he has provided for you. Honestly answer these questions: *Have you forgotten how good God has been to you? Have you been selfish and stubborn in your heart toward God for things you want or even just to get to your addiction?* It's okay to be honest here; God wants your honesty so he can fix your heart, so you can see that he has been with you all along through it all.

I want to return to Psalms 78. Even when God has been with them, provided for them, and protected them, they still wanted to do their own thing and never truly repented and trusted God. In verse 32 (NLT), it says, "But in spite of this, the people kept sinning. Despite his wonders, they refused to trust him." My question to you is the same thing that God asked me when I was still indulging in my addictions. *How long is it going to be until you truly turn from this and trust me? How many more days or weeks or months or years are you going to live bound because you won't turn to me? When are you going to trust me and not lean on your own understanding?* Like we talked about in previous chapters, God is a gentleman. He will never just kick the door of your life and come in without you turning you to him and inviting him in. Many times in the past, I have seen in my own life when I would have rather stayed where I was, even if that meant I was bound, than put my faith in God because it would require me to change and would make me uncomfortable. Is that you today? *Are you staying in a bound place because that's what you are used to? Are you afraid of letting go and fully trusting God? Are you trying to control everything that is currently in your life?*

When repenting and turning to God, it is very important that we be willing to endure the discomfort and the losses. With your trust in God, everything is always going to be okay, even if it doesn't feel or seem like it.

Further on in this chapter, we see God begin to kill a few of the people of that group who were disobeying and rebelling against him. God got upset with them because they weren't acknowledging his goodness and his faithfulness to them. It was not until God started killing them or taking things from them that they finally began taking God seriously and repented. In verses 33-35 (NLT), it says, "So God cut their lives short with sudden disaster, with nothing to show for their lives but fear and failure. *When he cared for them they ignored him, but when he began to kill them, ending their lives in a moment, they came running back to God, pleading for mercy.* They remembered that God, the Mighty one was their strong protector, the Hero-God who would come to their rescue."

I'm not telling you this to scare you or make you think that God is mean. God is the exact opposite of mean, but when he wants to discipline the people he loves, he will begin to take things from them. Personally, in my own life, when I put my addiction or things that I liked doing that was not pleasing to God above him, I began losing things, and that hurt me to my core. God will begin to take things from you just to get your attention and show you that everything that you currently have in this life is all because of him. He will take things away from you and discipline you when he sees that you are willfully sinning and not caring about the consequences.

Will God literally kill you today? No, because we have Jesus. But God will literally let you go down the wrong road and hit rock bottom so he can teach you what you are doing is wrong and goes against him. He did the same thing with Pharaoh because he was so prideful that he felt he didn't need God. In Exodus 9:12 NLT, it says, "But the Lord hardened Pharaoh's heart." God will not leave you; he will go down the road with you or even meet you at the end of that road in your pain. He does this because he wants to show that you what you're doing is not what he wants for you. God wants the very best for all of us, and if we are outside of his will, he will always lead us back into it, even if that means him using losses and pain. *Are the things you're currently doing worth you losing what God has given to you? Are the things you're doing worth slowing down the purpose God has given you? Are the things you're doing worth you experiencing pain because you wouldn't listen to God?*

When these people finally recognized that God has been with them their entire lives, they repented and turned to God. But they did something that we have been talking about this entire chapter. *They did not truly repent in their hearts, they only repented because of the struggle they were experiencing, and they felt bad for doing the things that they did.* In verse 36, it says, "Nevertheless they flattered him with their mouths and lied to him with their tongues." Having been lost people or other things, this group of people still didn't feel the need to truly repent and turn to God and follow them with their heart." This sounds like many of us, but the amazing thing about this entire story is that God forgave them anyway and spared them from losing any more things or other people. In verse 37, it says, *"But he, the source of compassion and loving kindness, forgave their wickedness and did not destroy them; Many times he restrained his anger and not stir up all of His wrath."* God will forgive you every time you say you repent your sins. He will always have mercy on you because he knows you are human and will sin again. But is that all you want? Why not truly repent from the things you're doing and start loving God and serving him in truth? I want to encourage you to not be like this group of people. Truly come to God as you are, and repent fully and wholeheartedly to him. When you repent to him and actually mean it, the changes that you begin to see in your life are amazing.

Today God is calling you to repent your sins and to trust that he will forgive you and restore you of the things and people you lost. I want to personally encourage you today to let God in and let him do what he does best—that is, transform you into who he has created and called you to be no matter how things look right now. I am praying for you.

Prayer: Heavenly Father, forgive me of my sins. Forgive me for having a hardened heart and not acknowledging how truly good you have been to me. I wholeheartedly repent from my wrongdoings, and I want to serve you with all my heart. I ask that you transform my mind so that I can recognize when I am wrong or recognize when I am about to do something wrong. I ask that you show me your good, pleasing, and perfect will that you have for my life. I am yours, and I choose you. I ask that you help me have a true repentant heart and transform my motives. In Jesus name, Amen.

Chapter Eleven

HEAVEN AND HELL

I want to talk about something that needs to be talked about as we talk about addiction, bondage, and temptation. This topic is not a popular topic in the church or even in the world today, but it is very needed that we talk about it as we live in the end times. The fact of the matter is that one day, which we do not know when, our Lord and Savior Jesus Christ is returning to earth, and he will gather all the people who are his and will cast out all those who never accepted him or denied him. In Matthew 3:12 NLT, John the Baptist says, "He comes with a winnowing fork in his hands and comes to his threshing floor and gather his wheat into his threshing floor to sift what is worthless from what is pure. And he is ready to sweep out his threshing floor and gather his wheat into his granary, but the straw will burn up with a fire that can't be extinguished!"

There are two places that we all go when we die and leave this earth: heaven or hell. And my question to you is, *where are you going? If Jesus were to come back today, would you be ready for his return? Would he say that he knows you?* The reality of it is that Jesus is the Alpha and the

Omega. He is the beginning and the end. He is the final judge. And if any of us are not right with him and do not know him, he will cast us into the unquenchable fire. I am not telling you this to scare you or to make you choose Jesus based on fear. I am telling you this because from the bottom of my heart, I want you saved and to live eternity with God and not separated from him. I don't have to know you to tell you how heavy of a burden I have for you to make to Heaven. I truly care about your salvation and your soul after you leave this earth. The life that all of us are living is temporary, and we could all be gone tomorrow. In James 4:14 AMP, it says, "Yet you do not know [the least thing] about what may happen in your life tomorrow. [What is secure in your life?] You are merely a vapor [like a puff of smoke or a wisp of stream from a cooking pot], that is visible for a little while then it vanishes [into thin air]."

The life that we live is literally like a vapor, and we can be here one moment then gone at any given time. Waiting on the right time to choose Jesus is not the way to go. Waiting to get cleaned up first is not the right way to go. Those are all lies from the devil straight from the pit of hell. Why would the devil lie to you and tell you, "You should just wait and get cleaned up first," "You should just wait until the time is right to choose Jesus"? Because he knows if he can get you to wait and stall on choosing Jesus as your personal Lord and Savior, there is a chance that you may die and never choose salvation. The truth is that Jesus came to die for all sinners. *You think you're too far gone? Jesus died for that. You think you're not worthy enough of to be loved by God? Jesus died for that. You think your addiction is too messy and ugly to be in God's presence? Jesus died for that. Are you battling with shame because of the habits that you do behind closed doors or even out in the light? Jesus died for that. You feel like there is no way out of your mistakes and wrong choices? Well, guess what? Jesus died for that too. There is freedom found in Jesus.*

I want all of us to realize that our problems, sins, or weaknesses do not scare God away. They are not too much for God, nor are they too heavy for him to carry. When Jesus went to the cross, he was literally carrying the weight of the world's sin on his shoulders. Jesus was severely beaten, whipped, spat on, had a crown of thorns placed on his head, and was ridiculed. He knew no sin but became sin. In Mark 15:34 NLT, when Jesus was on the cross in excruciating pain, he called out to God, saying, "My God, My God, why have you forsaken me?" Why did Jesus ask God this? *Because Jesus was in the place of judgment that you and I should have been in.* The truth is that should have been all of us on that cross, receiving death and judgment the first time we ever sinned and broke God's law. But because God loves us so much, he sent his son Jesus on earth to die in our place. If you ever begin to ask yourself or question if Jesus really loves you, think about this. Jesus literally stepped down from Heaven and got off his throne where he was worshipped by angels day and night to come to earth in the form of a human being. He came to serve, love, and eventually die for people, knowing that there was a chance that we may never even choose him as our Lord and Savior. *Jesus died for you and I on a maybe.* He went to the cross and stayed on the cross, hoping that we would maybe choose him and salvation, that we may obtain eternal life. So what happens if we never repent, confess, and choose Jesus as our personal Lord and Savior? I want to talk about the place where people who do not choose him go—hell.

What is hell? In the Bible, hell is also known as Hades, Sheol, or Gehenna, and it is mentioned over fifty times. Jesus himself talked more about hell than he did Heaven, and he described it very vividly. When Jesus was on the earth, he would warn the people about hell and what is to come. The only way that we know what hell really is by reading the Bible, which is the true word of God. What is the Bible? What is the word of God? The Bible is Jesus himself. In John 1:1-2 NLT, it says, "In the beginning was the word and the word was with God and the word was God. He was in the beginning with God." If we read down to verse 14, it says, "And the word became flesh and dwelt among us and we beheld his glory. The glory as of the only begotten of the Father full of grace and truth."

Jesus Christ himself is truth, and our whole faith is based on him. So Christianity is based and built on what Jesus says and not what we feel like we want to believe. Let's talk about what hell is like according to the Bible. In Matthew 25:41 NLT, Jesus says, "Then we will also say to those on the left hand. Depart from me you cursed, *into the everlasting fire prepared for the devil and his angels."* There will be an everlasting fire that is prepared for the devil and his angels (demons), and if we were to end up in hell, we would not be alone. We would be with the devil himself and his demons forever. Let's go down to verse 46, where Jesus says, "And these will go away into *everlasting punishment* but the righteous into eternal life." Hell is also a place of eternal punishment for people who chose to live their life in sin. Also, in Matthew 13:49-50 NLT, Jesus says, "So it will be at the end of age the angels will come forth and separate the wicked from among the just and cast them into the furnace of fire. *There will be wailing and gnashing of teeth."* In hell, the people who never choose Jesus will eternally be suffering, wailing, and gnashing their teeth.

In Mark 9:43-47 NLT, Jesus says, "If your hand entices you to sin, let it go limp and useless. For it is better for you to enter maimed than to have your entire body thrown into hell, the place of *unquenchable fire.* This is where the maggots never die and the fire never goes out. And if your foot leads into sin, cut it off! For it is better to enter life crawling than to have both feet and be flung into hell. This is where the maggots never die and the fire never goes out. And if your eye causes you to sin, pluck it out! For it is better to enter into life with one eye than to be thrown into hell with two." Jesus is saying it is better for you to lose even parts of your own body than for you to be in hell with them if you are sinning. Jesus doesn't literally mean to cut off your body parts or hurt yourself; he is saying to turn from them and to choose him while you still can. In Matthew 25:30 NLT, Jesus repeats himself, saying, "And cast the unprofitable servant into the *outer darkness.* There will be weeping and gnashing of teeth." Why does Jesus say the outer darkness? Because hell is a place without God, and God is light. In 2 Thessalonians 1:9 NLT, it says, "These shall be punished with everlasting destruction. From the presence of the Lord and the glory of his power." Just for a second, imagine a place without God. All good things come from God, like grace, forgiveness, love, mercy, protection, and provision. Just imagine what hell would be like and you are separated from God; a dark place of punishment with the devil, his demons, the fire that never stops, wailing and gnashing of teeth that never stops. If we were to go there, we would be in a place without God and tormented for all eternity. Furthermore, in Matthew 10:28 NLT, Jesus says, "And do not fear those who kill the body but cannot kill the soul. But rather fear him who is able to destroy both soul and body in Hell." Both the body and the soul will both be tormented in hell." Now that we know what Jesus says about hell, let's talk about some more Bible verses.

In Revelation 21:8 NLT, it says, "But the cowardly, faithless, despicable, murderers, perverts, sorcerers, idolaters and all the deceivers will find their place in the lake of fire and sulfur, which is the second death." Anyone who *chooses* to live in sin and not choose Jesus will be judged by God. Yes, I did say *choose* because it is choice that all of us has to make. If we do not ever choose Jesus and live in sin, we will receive a punishment and will be without God, suffering for all eternity with no way out. Yes, God is love, and he does give us time to come to him, but he is also just. He is the ultimate judge, and he will judge all of us based on how we lived our lives. God knows all those secret sins. He knows our hearts, so yes, he will judge us. God is holy and perfect, and all of us have sinned against him and his law.

God did not even spare the angels that sinned against him, so he will not spare us from his righteous judgment. In 2 Peter 2:4 NLT, it says, "Now don't forget, God had no pity for the angels when they sinned but threw them into the lowest, darkest dungeon of gloom and locked them in chains, where they are firmly held until the judgement of torment." There are currently demons in hell that are in chains of darkness. There are also different degrees of punishment. In Revelation 20:12-13 NLT, it says, "I saw the dead, the lowly and the famous alike, standing before the throne. Books were opened, and then another book was opened: The Book of Life. The dead were judged by what they had done as recorded in the books. And the sea gave up the dead souls that were in it. Then death and the underworld gave up their dead, and all were judged according to what they had done." Jesus also talked about this in the parable of the wicked servant. In Luke 12:46-47, he says, "Let me tell you what will happen to him. His master will suddenly return at a time that shocks him, and will remove the abusive, selfish servant from his position of trust. He will be severely punished and assigned a portion with the unbelievers. Every servant who knows full well what pleases his master, yet who does not make himself ready and refuses to put his masters will to action, will be punished with many blows. But the servant who does not know his masters will and unwittingly does what is wrong will be punished less severely. For those who have received a greater revelation from their master are required a greater obedience. And those who have been entrusted with great responsibility will be held more responsible to their master."

If you are a Christian leader, it is very important that you teach the word of God in a truthful and balanced way; it will cause people to stumble. If you are a false preacher/minister, there will be the worst punishment imaginable come judgment day. In Matthew 18:6 AMP, Jesus says, "But whoever causes one of these little ones who believe in me to stumble and sin [by leading them away from my teaching], it would be better for him to have a heavy millstone [as large as one turned by a donkey] hung around his neck and to be drowned in the depth of the sea." Also, in 2 Peter 2:17 NLT, it says, "These people are dried-up riverbeds, waterless clouds pushed along by the stormy winds- the deepest darkness of gloom has been prepared." The worst part of hell is reserved for false teachers who are here on earth.

I'm sure that you are well aware of one of the most popular verses in the Bible, John 3:16, which says "For this is how much God loved the world- he gave his one and only, unique son as a gift. So now everyone who believes in him will never perish but experience everlasting life." The problem in the world today is that we choose to believe in Jesus and accept him into heart, but we stop there. In verse 17, it says, "For God did not send the Son into the world to judge and condemn the world [that is, to initiate the final judgment of the world], but that the world *might be* saved through him." Might be saved? What exactly does this mean? A lot of Christians say "I am saved," but from what? *My question to you is, do you really believe that Jesus lived and died for you? Or did you just choose him to have your free get-into-Heaven card?* In John 3:36 (AMP), it says, "He *who believes and trusts* in the son and accepts him [as Savior] has eternal life [that is, already possesses it; but he who does not believe the son and chooses to reject to him, [disobeying him and denying him as savior] will not see [eternal] life, but [instead the wrath of God hangs over him continually." Take a break on reading and truly ask yourself if you really believe that Jesus is who he is and that he truly died for your sins.

When Jesus took our sins on the cross, he also took God's wrath on him. That is why Jesus suffered so much on the way to and on the cross. If God did not spare his punishment on his son Jesus Christ, then he will not spare his punishment on us if we never believe in and trust Jesus. As stated earlier, yes, God is love, but he is also holy, and he is also just. God will not just let us into heaven if we are full of sin. You might say, "But, Darrian, I'm a good person," but my question to you is, have you ever lied? Have you ever stolen something? If you have sinned against God or broken his law one time, then you have broken all laws. In James 2:10 NLT, it says, "For the one who attempts to keep all of the law of Moses but fails in just one point has become guilty of breaking the law in every respect!" I want all of us to fully understand this truth: No one on this earth is truly good enough for God. We broke his holy law the first time we ever sinned. Yes we are all deserving of his wrath and his judgment, but the amazing thing is that God loved us so much that he gave us a way out from this punishment, which is through his Son Jesus Christ.

In Romans 3:23-26 NLT, it says, "For everyone has sinned, we all fall short of God's glorious standard. Yet, God in his grace, freely makes us right in his sight. He did this through Jesus Christ when he freed us from the penalty of our sins. For God presented Jesus as a sacrifice for sin. People are made right with God when they believe that Jesus sacrificed his life, shedding his blood. This sacrifice shows that God was being fair when he held back and did not punish those who sinned in times past." How amazing is that? The blood of Jesus Christ paid for your sins and mine. But the only way to obtain his forgiveness is through truly believing that Jesus truly did die for us.

Your works, the amount of money you make, your fame, the number of degrees you have, the kind of house you live in, the kind of car you drive mean nothing eternally if you have not accepted Jesus Christ as your Lord and Savior.

I want to talk about a story in the Bible told by Jesus about a rich man and Lazarus. In Luke 16:19-31 NLT, Jesus says, "There was a certain rich man who was splendidly clothed in purple and fine linen who lived each day in luxury. At his gate lay a poor man named Lazarus who was covered with sores. As Lazarus lay there longing for scraps from the rich man's table, the dogs would come and lick his open sores. Finally, the poor man died and was carried by the angels to sit beside Abraham at the heavenly banquet. The rich man also died and was buried and he went to the place of the dead. There in torment, he saw Abraham in the far distance with Lazarus at his side. The rich man shouted, 'Father Abraham, have some pity! Send Lazarus over here to dip the tips of his finger in water and cool my tongue. I am in anguish in these flames.' But Abraham said to him, 'Son remember that during your lifetime you had everything you wanted, and Lazarus had nothing. So now he is here being comforted and now you are in anguish. And besides, there is a great chasm separating us. No one can cross over to you from here, and no one can cross over to us from there.' Then the rich man said, 'Please Father Abraham, at least send him to my father's home. For I have five brothers and I want him to warn them so they don't end up in this place of torment.' But Abraham said, 'Moses and the prophets have warned them. Your brothers can read what they wrote.' The rich man replied 'No, Father Abraham! But if someone is sent to them from the dead, then they will repent of their sins and turn to God. But Abraham said 'If they won't listen to Moses and the prophets, they won't be persuaded even if someone rises from the dead.'"

I know this was a lot to read, so let's break it down in a brief summary together. I want all of us to realize that there are people on this earth who do have power and have prestige/status and may even make a lot of money. Whether he/she is a doctor, musician, actor/actress, president, famous celebrity, or whatever, their occupation and the amount of money that they made mean absolutely nothing now. The main thing that matters is if they accepted Jesus Christ into their hearts and knew him. I know this is scary and may have you feeling uncomfortable, but it is the truth.

The good news for all of us is that we are all still alive on earth. As you read this sentence and every second after that you are breathing is God giving us time to accept him as our Lord and Savior so that we may be saved and have eternal life. It is our choice at the end of the day. God gave all of us free will to choose things. I personally want to tell you at this moment to choose Jesus Christ so that you will be saved. Repent all your sins, and God will forgive all your sins. As we are speaking right now, he is waiting for you to choose him. In Revelation 3:20 NLT, Jesus says, "Look! I stand at the door and knock. If you hear my voice and open the door, I will come in, and we will share a meal together as friends." God is waiting for you at the door of your heart. Will you let him in? If you do, then I want you to pray this prayer out loud and mean it from your heart:

> *God, I need you. Come and change my life. I know that I have sinned against you, and the punishment for it is hell. But, God, I don't want to go to hell. And I know I can't save myself, but only you can through Jesus Christ. Jesus, thank you for taking my punishment on the cross. You suffered in my place, so I accept it. And I accept that you are my Lord. Forgive me for all the sins I have done against you, and make me a new person. I open the door of my heart. So please come in and start a fresh relationship with me. Thank you, Jesus, in your name. Amen.*

If you just prayed that prayer, you are now a child of God if you truly meant it. Now that you accepted him into your heart as your personal Lord and Savior, it does not stop here. Every day all of us should be striving/wanting to grow spiritually and learn more about God. I encourage you to read your Bible, attend church, meet with

Christians/small groups that are good brothers/sisters in Christ as you walk in this journey. I pray this chapter gave you some insight and knowledge about hell and that you can find rest knowing that you are a child of God. I am praying for you.

Chapter Twelve

RIGHTEOUSNESS

What does it mean to be righteous or to be made right to God? I want to continue our conversation that we ended on in the previous chapter. A lot of us probably have heard this word be said in church or have read it when we are studying our Bible, but what does it really mean? Righteousness is being morally correct and justifiable. Pretty much, to be righteous means to have right standing with God and to be justified before God. When we become righteous with God, we become a part of his family and now are his children and are able to come into his presence. *We do not have to earn it; there are no amount of good things/works that we can do that can buy us favor or right standing with God. We cannot be perfect enough to be made right by God. Perfection could never earn us salvation. As a matter of fact, the Bible says that our perfection and righteousness are like filthy rags to God.* This sounds amazing, right? What better life to have than being able to come to the God of the universe about anything and having a relationship with him? So how are we to be made right by God if we are sinners and live in a fallen world? *The answer is Jesus.*

In Romans 5:1 TPT, Paul says, *"Our faith in Jesus transfers God's righteousness to us and he now declares us flawless in his eyes. This means we can now enjoy true and lasting peace with God, all because of what our Lord Jesus, the Anointed one has done for us."* The day/moment you believe that Jesus Christ lived and walked this earth, died for your sins, and rose, you are saved. In Romans 10:9 NLT, Paul also says, "For if you publicly declare with your mouth that Jesus is Lord and believe in your heart that God raised him from the dead, you will experience salvation." *At this moment, I want to continue the confession that we stated last chapter. If you have not confessed that Jesus is Lord and that God raised him from the dead, stop reading and confess this statement, really mean it from your heart, and give your life to Jesus; it is the best decision you will ever make. Ready? One, two, three, go!*

Congratulations, you are now saved and have experienced salvation through Jesus Christ. You are now in the family of God with the Holy Trinity as an adopted child. Heaven is now rejoicing! I am beyond proud of you, but most importantly, God is proud of you. Now that you are saved, you have eternal life with God and can rest that whatever the enemy tries to throw at you or do to you will not prosper. In Isaiah 54:17 NLT, it says, "No weapon that is formed against you will succeed. And every tongue that rises against you will condemn. This [peace, righteousness, security and triumph over opposition] is heritage of the servants of the Lord. And this is their vindication from me, says the Lord." Today I want you to know that yes, weapons will be formed against you, you will have trials, you will be tested, and some days are going to be tougher than others. God never promised us an easy life; he promises us an eternal life with him. Rest knowing that any trials or things that the enemy tries may form, but they are not powerful enough to take away your salvation.

In order to keep a strong relationship with God and to be sure of your salvation, I want to encourage you to set a side time in your everyday life to spend time with God. The only way that your relationship with God will grow is through spending intentional time with him. As we talked about in previous chapters, if it were a friend or girlfriend/boyfriend, all of us would take out time to spend time with them, right? It is the same thing with God. With a solid relationship with God, he can give you things that no other human on this earth could possibly give. I'm not talking about material things, I mean, eternal things, like joy, peace, love, self-control, and living water. Having a relationship with God is the best relationship you can ever have. Not only does God want a relationship with you, but he also wants to be your friend (John 15:15 NLT). Yes, you read that right! The God of the universe wants to be your friend and wants a real, true, authentic relationship with you. Rest in the fact today that the same God who made the stars, gave life to all the animals, made the skies and the oceans, and breathed life into you wants a friendship/relationship with you. Nothing in this life can compare to that. I pray that you experience freedom from this chapter and know for a fact that you are truly saved and in the kingdom of God through Jesus Christ. I am praying for you.

Prayer: Heavenly Father, thank you for sending Jesus to die on the cross for me while I was still a sinner so that I can be able to have a relationship with you. Thank you for making me right and justified in your sight. Help me grow my relationship and trust in you. In Jesus name, Amen.

Chapter Thirteen

GRACE

Grace is one of the most amazing characteristics about our Heavenly Father. Grace is literally the only way that we are able to stand before God and be in his presence because all of us are sinners. If we are born again and are his children, we have the privilege to stand before him because he is the one who made us right in his sight. The grace of God is something that none of us can take credit for; he gives it to us every day because he loves us that much. The second that you believed that Jesus died on the cross for your sins and rose from the dead was when God saved you by grace.

We do not have to earn grace; it is a gift from God (Ephesians 2:8: NLT). He gives us grace for our mistakes and sins because he knows that we are going to mess up and fall into sin at times. In the Bible and even today, God uses some of the most sinful and imperfect people in very powerful ways all because of his grace. Don't believe me? *Adam was blame-shifter and never took responsibility. Eve had very little to no self-control. Cain murdered his brother. Noah was a drunkard. Abraham was old, a liar, and let other men walk off with his wife. Lot always chose to be around or hang out with sinners. Job had a faithless wife who cursed God and went bankrupt. Isaac lied about his marriage by concealing it. Rebekah was manipulative. Jacob was a cheater and a deceiver. Rachel was a thief. Reuben was a pervert who slept with his father's concubine (lower status wife). Moses has a speech impediment and a temper. Aaron formed an idol and worshipped it instead of God. Miriam was greedy, had a jealousy problem, and was a gossip. Peter had a temper and denied Jesus three times. David was a murderer and had an affair then lied about it. Jonah ran from God. Paul was a Pharisee who murdered Christians before becoming one. Gideon was insecure and doubted God. Martha worried all the time. Thomas doubted that Jesus was resurrected. Sara had a baby through her servant and was impatient. Elijah was moody and suicidal. Jeremiah and Timothy were young. Zacchaeus was short and greedy. The Samaritan woman was divorced. Naomi was a widow. The disciples fell asleep while praying with Jesus. Lazarus was dead. I was a liar, stole, and was addicted to pornography and nicotine/tobacco.*

Long before any of us were ever born or even thought of by our parents, God made and rearranged plans for us. This means that he saw our mistakes, he saw our slip-ups, he saw our addictions, he saw us battling with anxious thoughts/depression, and he factored all those things in for our purpose. If God has called you to do his work and have impact in this world, there is nothing you can do to escape it or mess it up. *Like we talked about in chapter two, God works* all *things for the good of those who love him.* God will chase you down; he will come looking for you, and he'll even come down in the pit with you. As a matter of fact, he will meet you where you run to. If you're still addicted to porn, he's going to be there on your mind. If you're still addicted to a drug or alcohol, he's going to be there on your mind. If you're still depressed or battling with anxious thoughts, he's going to be there on your mind.

When God was calling Jonah to go to Nineveh so he could use him to tell the people there that their sin is great and that judgment is coming, Jonah literally ran the other way from God and what he was telling him to do. In Jonah 1:3 NLT, it says, "But Jonah got up and *went in the opposite direction of the Lord."* Doesn't this sound like what we do? God shows us who we are in Christ and our purpose; he shows us that we can be free from the addiction, he shows us that we can break free from mental bondage, he shows us that he's bigger than our problems, but a lot of the times we run back to the thing that has us bound because we are afraid of stepping out and doing what God said to do. If that is you today, I want to challenge you to stop running back to what has had you bound. *If God is choosing you, that means he is going to chase after you, even if you rebel. If God is showing you something, that means that he is trying to do something.*

Although Jonah went in the opposite direction of God, look at what our Heavenly Father does. In verse 17, it says, "Now the Lord *had arranged* for a great fish to swallow Jonah. And Jonah was inside the fish for three days and three nights." God literally met Jonah where he ran to and put him a place where it was only them two. Then while in the fish, Jonah prayed to God and finally went to Nineveh and did what God told him to do.

Why am I telling you this story, and how does it all relate to grace? The fact that God met Jonah where he went just shows that God not only graciously picks us, but he also comes after us. He could have easily picked someone else or just let Jonah go and hide. But God came after Jonah and still allowed him to go preach at Nineveh because God graced him for his purpose. Even when Jonah did not pick God, God picked Jonah, and he does the same exact thing with us. In Ephesians 1:4 NLT, the apostle Paul says, "Even before he made the world, *God loved us and chose us in Christ* to be holy and without fault in his eyes." It does not matter where you run to or how far you run; you cannot outrun God's grace. The assignment/purpose that God has for you is wrapped in grace; all we have to do is accept it. *It does not matter how things look now, how you start, or even the process of you becoming who you are. It is never about how you start; it is about how and where you end up. Rest in the fact today that your purpose and everything else that God has for you is covered by his amazing grace.*

Now what do we do if we have rebelled and turned our backs on God? How can we come to him to tell him sorry and that we're ready to be used? How can we make up for the time that was lost when we weren't doing what God told us to do? How can we accept the gift of

God's grace? As children of God, all of us can go to God boldly and passionately with a humble heart in prayer. In Hebrews 4:15 NLT, it says, "So let us come boldly to the throne of our gracious God. There we will receive his mercy, *and we will find grace to help us when we need it most.*" As children of God, we can *always* go to his throne with passionate prayer anytime of the day. I strongly believe that when we come before God, he does not want us to come to him fearful, with our head down or our tail tucked between our legs. He wants us to come to him with fervent, passionate prayer and a humble heart. Doing this is acknowledging that he is the Lord of lords and that he is who he says he is.

When we go to God with passion and humility in our hearts, God longs to give grace to his children. In James 4:6 NLT, it says, "And he gives grace generously. As the scriptures say, *'God opposes the proud but gives grace to the humble.'*" One thing that God does not like are people with proud hearts. God cannot help, extend grace, or bless us if our hearts are proud. If we never confess or see that we are wrong and we need him every day, how can God bless us?

When we come before him in prayer, yes, be bold and pray with fire, but always make sure that your heart is humble. God literally views pride as the opposite of him, and he counts that as you being against him. As a matter of fact, pride is the original sin. We can all go to God in prayer, ask him all these things, pray for wisdom or guidance, but if God sees that we are being prideful in our hearts, he will not listen to us. In Job 35:12 NLT, it says, "And when they cry out, God does answer because of their pride." Like we've been talking about in this entire book, it is very important that you are honest not only with yourself, but also with God. Being humble in the presence of God is showing him that we acknowledge his sovereignty and that we can do nothing outside of him.

In 2 Chronicles 7:14 NLT, the Lord himself says, "Then if my people who are called by name will *humble themselves and pray and seek my face and turn from their wicked ways,* I will hear from heaven and forgive their sins and restore their land." I don't know about you, but this verse gives me such a peace of mind because God promises to not only forgive us but to also restore us of everything that we may have lost because of our rebellion. As you see in this verse, yes, God promises us two things, but in order to receive his promise, it requires us to do some things as well. I want to walk through this verse step-by-step.

The first thing that God says to do in this verse is to humble ourselves. As we have been talking about in these last few paragraphs, it is crucial that all of us humble ourselves before the Lord. In 1 Peter 5:6 NLT, Peter says, *"So humble yourselves under the mighty power of God,* and at the right time he will lift you up in honor." The Lord will always be ready to answer or help us if our hearts are humbled before him. If you haven't humbled yourself or have truly acknowledged that some of the things that you have been doing are wrong, take a break on reading and truly reflect on your heart's posture. The most dangerous thing is when we are praying to God but we fail to realize or see that we really are wrong or are in need of him. If we never acknowledge our wrongs and humbly go to God, how will we ever grow or change?

The second thing that God says to do in this verse to pray and seek his face. All the answers to our problems are only found in God, not in anyone else. Like we talked about in previous chapters, the only way to hear back or receive things from God is if we pray to him. In Matthew 6:6 NLT, Jesus says, "But when you pray, go away by yourself, shut the door behind you and pray to your Father in private. Then your Father, *who sees everything will reward you."* After we humble ourselves and pray to seek his face, God will immediately reward us with his amazing gift of grace. God wants to hear from us so that he can extend us his grace; he does not want us to sit in depression, regret, sorrow or anxiety. If you have not prayed to God recently about some things you have been doing or even things you are going through, I want to strongly encourage you to pause on reading and pray to our Father.

The third and final step God says to do in this verse is to turn from our wicked ways. Another word for "wicked ways" is our sins. This goes back to the chapter where talked about repentance. Simply turning from our sins and the way that we have been doing things is what repentance is. The second that we have turned and put our focus back on God is when we reestablish our connection with him. God doesn't want us facing away from him and into sin because that is when we typically begin to stray away from him, and eventually, the relationship that we once had with God will begin to fade away. I want to encourage you, if you still haven't repented, to go to God with a truthful heart and repent your sins and wrongdoings so you can reestablish connection with him.

Now that we have completed those three steps that God says to do, that is when we can accept the amazing gift of grace! You are worthy of receiving grace; you do not have to do anything extra or work to receive it. If I am being honest, it is only by the grace of God that I am able to type this book and tell you the things that I have been through, things that I have learned in my walk with God and where I am at now. You can experience this same exact grace and live fully in the purpose that he created you for if you accept this gift. It is one of the best decisions you will ever make in this life on earth. I hope that in this chapter, you learned what grace is and how to accept it and walk in it. I hope this chapter gives you hope that no matter where you are or what you are going through, the grace of God is bigger than all those things. I am praying for you.

Prayer: Heavenly Father, thank you. Thank you for your amazing gift of grace that you offer me every single day that I wake. Thank you for graciously choosing me before I chose you. I ask that, as I continue on my walk with you, you extend me grace of my shortcomings. I ask that your grace carries me into my purpose and continues to stay with me as I walk in my purpose. I humbly admit and confess that I need you, and outside of you, I can do nothing. In Jesus name, Amen.

Chapter Fourteen

FORGIVENESS

What exactly does it mean to truly forgive someone? Psychologists generally define "forgiveness" as a conscious, deliberate decision to release feelings of resentment or vengeance toward a person or group that has harmed you, regardless of whether they deserve your forgiveness. I know what you're thinking here, "Do I really need to forgive that person who did me wrong?" "Do I really have to forgive that ex who cheated on me and lied to me?" "Do I have to forgive that family member who molested me when I was younger?" Do I really need to forgive the people who introduced me to the drug or addiction that I battle with today?" "Do I really need to forgive the people who laughed at my dreams or passion?" "Do I really need to forgive the people who made fun of me and laughed at me?" "Do I really need to forgive my parents for not noticing me or seeing my hurt?" The answer to all these questions are yes. In order for God to forgive us of our sins and our daily failures, it requires us to forgive those who have wronged us.

Don't believe me? In Matthew 6:14-15 NLT, Jesus says, *"If you forgive those who sin against you, your heavenly Father will forgive you. But if you refuse to forgive others, your Father will not forgive your sins."* I want all of us to realize that God does not have to forgive us of our sins. He is not obligated to show us forgiveness because we sinned against him first, and he is sovereign. But because of his endless and reckless love for us, he chooses to forgive us every time we fall or sin against him. Yes, the pain that you felt from people you care about is real. Yes, they were wrong for what they did or spoken over you, and no, they might not deserve your forgiveness. But the sobering fact that all of us need to understand is that none of us deserve God's forgiveness. But God chooses to because of what Jesus did on the cross for us. Every time we fall, every time we feel anger in our heart, every time we feel resentment toward someone, every time we indulge in the addiction that we struggle with, every time we become prideful, every time we are lazy, every time we intentionally sin, every time we even doubt God, he forgives us. So as children of God, it is expected of us to forgive the people who have wronged us.

You might be asking, "Well, how many times do I have to?" "If I forgive them four times and they keep doing the same thing, I might as well just stop forgiving them because they obviously aren't taking me seriously, right?" Just for a second, think about how many times you fall short and sin against God. We sin literally every single day, whether we know it or not, and God still ends up forgiving us, even when we do not ask him. This reminds me of when Peter asked Jesus how many times he should forgive someone who has sinned against him. The answer that Jesus told Peter blew me away. In Matthew 18:21-22 NLT, it says, "Then Peter came to him and asked 'Lord, how often should I forgive someone who sins against me? Seven times?" Then Jesus replies, *"No, not seven times. But seventy times seven." If you are like me and not good at math, Jesus says to forgive the person who sins against you a total of 490 times.* But the question is, how often?

My question to you is, does it matter how often? Jesus never said 490 times per minute, per hour, per day, per month, or per year. What Jesus is saying here is forgive them more than they sin against you. You doing so will reflect his character and nature on to others.

When people intentionally/knowingly wrong you and you forgive them, even though they do not deserve it, shows that you are a child of God. Forgiving others when they wrong us is not for them; it is for us. The fact of the matter is other people do not block our blessings. Majority of the time we block our own blessings because of the hardness of our hearts. Forgiveness allows us to be free in our hearts and minds. If we continue to live and not forgive people, all we would be doing is blocking our own blessings that God has for us. Or even worse, we would be carrying around the weight of unforgiveness, and that would begin to affect us more than it affects the people who wronged us. It would eventually begin to affect our everyday lives, our functioning, and would make us bitter toward everybody we talk to. It would create trust issues internally, and we could miss the blessing in people God placed in our lives.

At this moment, I want you to write down a list people whom have hurt you or you know that you feel anger or resentment toward. After you do that, I want you take a break on reading and forgive them in your heart. I would hate for you to continue to live your life every day carrying baggage and blocking your own blessings. I want to see you happy, I want to see you whole, I want to see you free, I want to see you walking into the blessings that God has for you, and most importantly, I want you to be forgiven by God.

Now that we've talked about forgiving others, I want to talk about something that I personally struggle with and that some of you may struggle with too—forgiving yourself. Yes, we all make mistakes, we stumble, we fall, and we make wrong turns in life. That happens, and it is inevitable for it not to happen. If you are struggling with forgiving yourself and are in bondage because of shame and guilt, I know exactly what you are going through, and you're not alone in that struggle. I know what it is like to be so hard on yourself and not even feel worthy enough to be in God's presence or even be used by God. I know what it is like struggling to even look at yourself in the mirror. Today I want you to rest in this fact: The moment you get in the presence of God and asks for forgiveness, he instantly forgives you. As a matter of fact, he forgave you before you even came to him with tears in your eyes. He knows what you're going to ask or say before you even ask or say it.

I know it's hard to believe that God forgives you immediately because you find it hard to even forgive yourself. Brother or sister, I want you realize this simple fact: You will never be perfect as long as you are here on earth. None of us will be perfect until the day Jesus Christ returns. God knows that you are going to mess up, fall, and sin. We are all human and live in a fleshly body. No, that does not excuse you to sin or just do whatever you want to do. It means that you are human and will make mistakes, but thank God for his amazing grace that never runs out. Today, at this moment, if you are struggling with forgiving yourself and are in bondage because of self-guilt or even condemnation, I want you to stop reading and forgive yourself for your mess-ups and failures. There is so much freedom when you forgive yourself and do nothing but be still and accept the grace that God freely gives you.

I hope that this chapter gave you some insight and encouragement to forgive others so that God will forgive you. I hope you begin to forgive yourself of the things you have done and walk in the grace that God freely gives you. I am praying for you.

Prayer: Father, forgive me for not forgiving the people who have hurt or done bad things to me. Help me to forgive others so that I may experience your forgiveness and grace. Also, help me forgive myself of my sins and my failures, and help me realize that I can never be perfect but with you, I can have peace knowing that I am already forgiven by you. In Jesus name, Amen.

Chapter Fifteen

FRUITS OF THE SPIRIT

When you begin to walk with Jesus and begin to trust him as your personal Lord and Savior, the Holy Spirit begins to work in you what is of the Spirit, which is good. The only problem that every Christian has that is alive and currently breathing is our flesh and our nature to want to sin or to want the things that this world has to offer us. As we have talked about in the chapters about temptation, we cannot beat the flesh or want things that are opposite of the flesh without the power of the Holy Spirit. What all of us should be wanting to gain or produce are the fruits of the Spirit. In Galatians 5:22-23 NLT, the apostle Paul says, *"The Holy Spirit produces this kind of fruit in our lives: love, joy, peace, patience, kindness, goodness, faithfulness, gentleness, and self-control."*

Now what does Paul mean by "fruit"? Does he mean that we look good like delicious fruit growing in a garden or on a tree? No, what Paul is saying is the way we treat people, the way we look at other people or ourselves, the things we do or even how feel should only come from the Holy Spirit and nothing else. In Matthew 16:20

NLT, Jesus says, "Just as you can identify a tree by its fruit, so you can identify people by their actions." Your everyday decisions, actions, habits, or things you want in life all determine whether or not you are led by the Spirit or your flesh because things of the Spirit reflect the nature of Jesus and things of your flesh or selfish wants reflect the wants of this world. I want to discuss all nine fruits of the Spirit with you and talk about how they all relate to addiction, bondage, or temptation.

Fruit of the Spirit no. 1: Love. As human beings, all of us want to feel love or be loved in some way, shape, or form. Many of us go to people who are not good for us, have sex with multiple people, watch pornography and masturbate to fill the void where do not feel loved, which has the power to eventually turn into an addiction. *Regarding pornography, statistics show that 76 percent of eighteen- to twenty-four-year-old Christians actively seek out porn, and over forty million Americans are regular visitors to porn sites.* I can tell you personally I was a part of these statistics and I was extremely addicted to pornography. I know exactly what it is like to try and find love from pornography and masturbation. Not only that I know what it is like to try and find love from having sex with multiple people. Me always being made fun of about my speech impediment, me not feeling attractive to women, and me being turned down drove me to porn and sex instead of the presence of God.

The only place that you truly find real love is through a relationship and in the presence of God. *God loves you wholeheartedly, not just because he is God, but also because God is love (1 John 4:8: NLT).* God is the literal definition of love; love is not found in a person or a habit. God loved all us so much that he sent his one and only Son to die on the cross for us so that we can have eternal life and have a relationship with him built on him, built on love. If you are having issues or struggling with low self-esteem, self-confidence, or realizing your true worth, rest in the fact that if no one in this world loves you, you have a God who is in heaven who loves you far beyond words can describe. In Psalms 115:12 AMP, it says, *"The Lord who is [always] thinking about us,* will bless us." God loves you so much that he thinks about you each and every day, even when you are not thinking about him. Today, at this moment, I want to encourage you to invite the love of God into your heart. Pause on reading if you have to because the love of God is greater than anything that is in this world.

Fruit of the Spirit no. 2: Joy. Joy is another emotion or feeling that all of us as human beings want to have. Many times we try going to things like people, a career, the amount of money we make, vacations, the number of degrees we have, accolades, how many clubs/organizations we are in, how many Instagram or Facebook followers we have, how many people see our progress, and the approval of others. *Brother or sister, joy only comes from the Lord and only him.* Nothing in this world can bring true joy that will satisfy your heart. That is why you see people who have more degrees than a thermometer, making $300,000+ a year, and have a big house but hurt and are miserable on the inside. The things that a lot of people in this world care about can never fully bring them joy that makes them feel full or complete. True joy satisfies the heart in a way that temporary happiness never can. In Psalms 4:7 NLT, it says, *"You have put more joy in my heart than they have when their grain and wine abound."* No amount of money, power, prestige, education, or material things in this world is going to bring you more joy than God.

Honestly, everything that we gain or that we have while we are here on earth means absolutely nothing when we compare them to God and spending eternity with him. In Ecclesiastes 1:2-3, 8 NLT, it says, *"Everything is meaningless, completely meaningless! What do people get for all their hard work under the sun? Everything is wearisome beyond description. No matter how much we see, we are never satisfied. No matter how much we hear, we are not content."* All of us can work hard and do everything under the sun to become very successful, but if we do not have an active and true relationship with God, we will never experience true joy that is only from him. Today I want to challenge you to put aside your degrees, your job, your busy schedule, the amount of money you make, the amount of Instagram followers you have, your status or popularity and seek God for true joy. Joy that is in the world does not compare even the slightest bit to the joy that you gain from our Father in heaven.

Fruit of the Spirit no. 3: Peace. What is it that you do to get peace? What is your escape route from the realities or stresses of this life? Do you smoke? Do you drink? Do you watch porn? Do you have pride? Do you gossip? Do you lie? Do you have sex? Do you binge eat? Do you go on a shopping spree? At this moment, I want you to pause on reading and take a second to truly reflect on what it is you do to feel peace when you are overwhelmed, stressed, or worried. One day, as I watching a sermon and hearing the pastor speak, the Holy Spirit said something so profound to me, I knew he was talking directly to me that day.

When the pastor said, *"Anything that you get peace from that is not of God is a counterfeit."* I immediately identified the things that I was going to for peace instead of God. And maybe that is you at this moment. I want you to realize and see that whatever it is you do to get your buzz, high, or fix is only a temporary thing that satisfies your flesh. But like we talked about in previous chapters, the flesh is never satisfied, so what we do as humans is we continue to indulge more and more until we feel as if we are satisfied, which eventually turns into you becoming addicted. As you know, the thing that you indulge in gives you the thrill and covers your feelings that you feel for a temporary moment, then it goes away, and you are back to the feelings that drove you to indulge in what satisfies you.

With Jesus, you never have to feel like you are unsatisfied because his Spirit is so powerful that it will block out what your flesh desires and you will feel whole. One of my favorite stories in the Bible is when Jesus talks to a Samaritan woman at the well. The woman was coming to draw water from a well to satisfy her physical needs because she was literally thirsty. But then Jesus offers her water that will never make her thirsty again, which is himself. In John 4:13 NLT, Jesus says, "Anyone who drinks this water will soon become thirsty again. *But those who drink the water that I give will never be thirsty again.* It becomes a fresh, bubbling spring within them, giving them eternal life."

You may be going to the things that you enjoy doing to fulfill your temporary discomfort and that satisfies your flesh just like the Samaritan women did, but until you truly give yourself and struggle over to Jesus, you will never be satisfied. I can personally tell you no amount of the thing or things that you indulge in will bring you peace. It is a never-ending cycle that does nothing but continues to hurt you spiritually. I want to personally encourage you today to let go of what you do to fulfill your own desires and to let Jesus fill those spots. Yes, it is going to feel uncomfortable and weird at first, but when Jesus fills your heart and spirit with his Spirit, you begin to fell peace that is out of this world.

Fruit of the Spirit no. 4: Patience. We live in a world today that everything is fast-paced and everything has to be done now. We go on social media, and we see our friends, family, or people who we even do not know, and we compare our journey/process to theirs, and we think that we are behind in life. *Did you know that comparison of yourself can be just as dangerous as being addicted to something and can create mental bondage?* There is a reason why God does not give or show us everything that we ask him for in this life all at once. He wants us to patiently wait and trust that if we put our faith in him, everything is going to be okay and doors will open as they should and that we will most certainly spend eternity with him in Heaven. But in the process of waiting on God, he knows that we are all too human and that through us not being patient, we will do things like sin, move in haste, or try to do extra things to "help God" because we could not wait on him.

In 2 Peter 3:9 NLT, it says, "The Lord isn't really being slow about his promise, as some people think. No, *he is being patient for your sake.* He does not want anyone to be destroyed, but wants everyone to repent." I want us to realize the power of this verse. Peter is not talking about worldly things in this verse. Yes, there are assignments and things on this earth that God wants you to do and places that he will place you. *But ultimately, his promise is that you get into Heaven and spend eternity with him. That is why this verse finishes with him saying that he wants everyone to repent.* Remember, all the word "repentance" means is to turn to God. *God cannot give you his promise if you have not turned to him and patiently wait on him to do what he is trying to do.*

I'll put it this way: Imagine you have your back turned to your friend or family member and they are trying to give you something. It would be much harder for him/her to give you the thing they have for you because you would have to blindly reach back and try to get it with your hand and you will have no sense of direction. It would be much easier if you turned around and faced them so that you may receive what it is they have for you with a better and sure sense of direction. It is the same thing with God.

If we are going through this life with our backs turned to God and have no sense of direction, we are pretty much walking blind, not knowing how to receive the things that God ultimately planned for us to receive. But if we were to turn to God through repentance, we now have a sense of direction of how to walk and receive what God has for us. That is why God is so patient with us and wants us to be patient with him. The things he has for you and eternal life are yours to have, but receiving the promises of God is a process. Today I want to challenge you to repent and have patience with God and trust that everything is going to turn out the way that it should.

Fruit of the Spirit no. 5: Kindness. As human beings, all of us are called to be kind and to show love to one another. In Ephesians 4:32 NLT, it says, "Be kind to each other, tenderhearted, forgiving one another, just as God through Christ has forgiven you." But as we all know, it is very hard to show kindness, love, or forgiveness to the people who have hurt us, broken our heart, stabbed us in the back, used us, lied to us, manipulated us, or even abused us. Yes, those things may have hurt you deep to your core, and you have every reason to be upset or hurt, but God has called all of us to show kindness and love to our enemies. As a matter of fact, Jesus says to pray for our enemies and to turn the other cheek if someone hits you. If you have been wronged or hurt by a friend, family member, coworker, or even a stranger, I know exactly what that feels like, and let me tell you, not showing hinders you from growing, and it can actually harden your heart and make you bitter, which can cause bondage in itself.

I began to find myself being very bitter to everybody I knew and even people I did not know. My heart had gotten so hard that I lost myself in the unforgiveness that I would give people. *If that is you today, I want to personally tell you to let go of what people have done to you, spoken over you, made fun of you about, abused you physically, mentally, or physically and forgive them. If you never forgive them, all that is going to do is turn you so bitter to the point where you won't even listen to God.*

As my relationship with God grew deeper, I learned something that blew my mind: *Hurt people hurt people. People who do not know themselves, love themselves, or who have low self-confidence are the people who hurt people.* It's not that they are bad people; they just have personal heart issues that have yet to be resolved or fixed by God. So what I learned was, instead of not forgiving them or extending kindness and showing love, to do the opposite. When people hurt me, I learned to flip what is normal in today's culture. I found myself loving the people who have wronged me, praying for those who did me wrong, and showing kindness even though they did not deserve it. When I started to do that, *God began to show me that is what he does with all of us every single day. He extends his love, protects us, and shows us mercy and kindness, even though we do not deserve it.* When you love people who wronged you all because they do not know themselves, you are showing that God and his Spirit dwells inside of you. You showing love and kindness, even though they don't deserve it, does not exemplify you, it actually exemplifies God, and that will cause the person to turn to God and get help with what they are struggling with. Today I want you to challenge yourself to forgive the people who have hurt you and show them love. If you need to, take a break from reading and pray to our Father.

Fruit of the Spirit no. 6: Goodness. God is good to us each and every day we are alive, plain and simple. Every day God shows us his goodness in small ways that we take for granted and big ways that are clear and that we should praise him for. Every morning God wakes us up; the fact that we have a roof over our heads and clothes on our back and our current health status are all ways that God shows his goodness to us. Even in the midst of our suffering and bad choices,

God still always provides because goodness is a part of God's nature; that's just who he is. In Exodus 33: 19 NLT, God says, *"I will make my goodness pass before you and I will call out my name before you. For I will show mercy to anyone I choose, and I will show compassion to anyone I choose."*

Because we are his children and God lives in us through the Holy Spirit, he also wants us to be good. By being good, God wants us to serve others out of love, give to those who cannot pay us back, grant others mercy, and do things *out of love and not out of obligation.* In Matthew 5:48 NLT, Jesus says, *"But you are to be perfect, even as your Father in Heaven is perfect."* Now wait a minute. How are we supposed to be perfect? How are we supposed to be perfect like the all-knowing, sovereign God who is seated above the entire earth? The reality of it is that we cannot be perfect apart from Jesus and the Holy Spirit. What Jesus means is that we should reflect God's goodness and nature onto other people. When people meet you or are talking to you, it should get to a point to where they see God's reflection upon you. They should be able to hear him through your speech and the way you carry yourself.

The way you speak, the way you give, the way you serve, and the way you love have very little to do with you. Everything you do that other people see always exposes if you are truly filled with his Spirit and will always bring his name glory. No matter your struggle, pain, addictions you struggle with, or mental bondage, one thing all of us can do each and every day is reflect the goodness of the Lord to other people. Today I want to encourage you to show goodness to others, no matter what you are going through. You can be the answer someone's prayer and show them that God sees and hears them, but it all starts with you submitting to God and his Spirit so his goodness can flow through you.

Fruit of the Spirit no. 7: Faithfulness. Have you ever had somebody promise you something, but they couldn't keep their word? Have you ever had someone tell you something, but they end up doing the exact opposite of what they told you? Well, brother and sister, the God we serve is the complete opposite of that. God is a man of his word, and anything that he speaks in the atmosphere, he will accomplish, and he will always keep his promises. Here are just a few of God's promises that are for all of us: *He will fight for you. He will renew your strength. He will always be with you and never forsake you. No weapon formed against you shall prosper. You are free from darkness. He will forgive your sin. He satisfies your desires with good things. His love is abounding. He will pour out his Spirit on all. He hears your prayer. He will make your paths straight. He will give you comfort. He will come near to you. He will meet your needs. He works for your good. He will bless you. You belong to him as a child. God will remain in you. The Holy Spirit will guide you to all truth. God will make you strong and firm. You are under grace. His love is everlasting. He protects you from evil. With him, nothing is impossible. You are redeemed. He will deliver you. He is your shield. He will finish the work he began in you. He will never let the righteous fall. He will watch over you. You are chosen, holy, and loved.*

God is not a God who breaks his promises; God is a God who will do anything to accomplish his promises in your life because he loves you that much. God is faithful, even when we are faithless. God is faithful, even when we may make bad decisions and fall into sin. God is faithful, even when we doubt him and who he is. God is faithful during your storm. God is faithful, even if you are still addicted. God is faithful, even if you are still battling temptation. God is faithful, even when you are battling with anxiety/depression and are in mental bondage. As we have been talking about in the majority of this book, God will never leave nor forsake you, even in the middle of your problems.

In 2 Timothy 2:13 NLT, it says, *"If we are unfaithful, he remains faithful, for he cannot deny who he is."* Today rest in the fact that there is nothing you can do to push the faithfulness that God offers us away. Faithfulness is a part of God's nature; that is a part of who he is. God wants to be faithful to us; he wants to provide for us, he wants to be there for us in our time of distress, he wants to comfort us when we are mourning/hurting, he wants to forgive us and cleanse us, but it all starts with us trusting that God is faithful and that he truly is who he says he is. I know it may be hard to have faith at times, especially when you are stuck in bad habits or mental bondage. I have been there, and I know the feeling all too well. *One thing I had to realize and believe in my own heart was God is not a human being.*

I believe a lot of times what we do is compare God to human beings when we mess up or do something that we know is wrong. We think that God is going to rebuke us or push us away or even say "Don't talk to me." We think that there is no way we could ever go to God because of our addictions or our anxious thoughts. No, God does not like sin nor tolerate sin, and there will always be consequences for our sin, but God 100 percent definitely wants to us to go to him and vent to him about what we are currently facing. If you are reading this, I want you to know that you can go to God about the things you are facing because he already knows. God knows our struggles and things we go through before they even happen to us. That is why he wants us to come to him and trust that he is faithful to help us with anything. Today I want to encourage you to let go of what you think or even feel about God and to trust his faithfulness toward you as a son or daughter.

Fruit of the Spirit no. 8: Gentleness. When we bring our problems to God, he does not and will never rebuke us out of his presence. As children of God, God loves all of us deeply and wants to help us with whatever it is that we are going through. I want to talk about one of my favorite parables that Jesus told in the Bible: "The Prodigal Son." This parable that Jesus taught is one of the most powerful pieces of scripture to me because not only is that so many Christians today, but also, that was me a little over year ago.

In this parable, Jesus says that one of two sons of a father went away from home and took everything he owned with him. While being away from his father in this place, the son wasted all his money and was living wild. Not only did the son lose all his money, but also, a famine came and struck the land. He began to starve because he had no money and could not get anything to eat. Things got so bad that he actually got a job on a farm, but that still could not satisfy what he was really missing in his life. He was all alone and still nobody gave him anything or helped him. I want to stop on talking about the prodigal and discuss with you how this relates to us.

When we stray away from God in our life, we think we will be okay, stand strong on our own, or even provide for ourselves, but the truth is we can't. Put yourself in the shoes of the prodigal son. He strayed away from his father, lost everything that his father gave him out of love, then had to do things in his own power just to get a job so he can survive. Does this sound familiar to you? *Have you strayed away from God because he hasn't answered your prayers yet? Have you strayed away from God because things didn't go the way you wanted them to? Have you strayed away from God because of the shame from your addiction? Have you strayed away from God because of your anxiety/depression? Take a moment and truly think about where you are at in life and truly ask yourself if you are in a right relationship with God.*

Let us return to the parable. After the son saw that he could no longer do things for himself and in his own power, he decided to go home. In Luke 15:18-19 NLT, Jesus says that the boy said, "I will get up and go to my father and say to him, Father I have sinned against heaven and in your sight. I am no longer worthy to be called your son." Doesn't this sound like us when we go to God in prayer when we have been so distant from him? I can personally tell you I have been struggling with this for years now. If you are feeling unworthy of even being in God's presence, I know exactly what that feels like. But just like God accepted me and made me right, he will do the same exact thing for you. You are always welcomed into his presence through Jesus Christ.

In chapter 15 verse 20 (NLT), Jesus says, "So he got up and came to his father. *But while he was still a long way off, his father saw him and was moved with compassion for him, and ran and embraced him and kissed him.*" How amazing is this to you? *No matter what you have done or even thought, God has had his eyes on you from a far distance, and when he sees you seeking him through prayer and reading the Bible, he fully accepts you with open arms. He does not rebuke you for straying off from him. Our Heavenly Father is so gentle with us, even when we do wrong, because he loves us that much.* Today I want to encourage you to rest in the fact that God, with his gentleness, accepts you as you are and wants you to talk to him about what has happened in your life.

Fruit of the Spirit no. 9: Self-Control. When it comes to self-control, our flesh hates it. As humans beings, we do not like needing to have self-control over our thoughts, actions, or habits. As we have talked about in previous chapters, our flesh and the Holy Spirit are always clashing because, as humans, we do not want to do what the Spirit wants us to do because, by nature, all of us want to sin. Self-control is a discipline that God grows in us when we continually choose to die to our flesh and live in him. I want to return to a verse that we talked about in previous chapters: Romans 7:18 (NLT). It says, "For I know that good itself does not dwell in me, that is, in my sinful nature. For I have the desire to do what is good, but I cannot carry it out."

Isn't it frustrating to know what is right and still not being able to do it? This is the main thing I struggled with in my entire season of repeatedly doing the same thing over and over. Maybe you're there today and you're wanting to know how to obtain true self-control. So what is the missing piece between our knowledge action? *The answer is Jesus.* The fact and reality is sin runs deep inside of us, but as Christians, we have the One in us who can give us the strength to have self-control. We do not have the strength on our own to be able to choose what is right, especially when it does not feel good.

Self-control is only gained through us spending personal time with God and letting him heal the areas where we are weak at. No, it may not feel good at the moment or during the process of us learning self-control, but eventually, we will learn how to say no to our flesh and yes to God and obey what he says. Today I want to encourage you to let go of your control and begin to spend time with God so that he may teach you self-control.

I pray that this chapter helped you understand more about the fruits of the Spirit and that you begin to spend time with God so that you know how to apply them in your everyday life. I am praying for you.

Prayer: Heavenly Father, as I seek a relationship with you and grow in you, I ask that you teach me all the fruits of your Spirit. Help me activate the faith to put into practice all the things that you teach me in my everyday life. I confess and I admit that I cannot produce the fruit you want me to outside of the Holy Spirit. Thank you for loving me for me, and thank you that I can be able to have a relationship with you through Jesus Christ. I am all yours. In Jesus name, Amen.

Chapter Sixteen

STOP GOING BACK

What is it that God has delivered you from time and time again, yet you still keep going back to it? Whether it be a bad habit, substance, pornography, or negative thinking, I find that we get the deliverance that God wants us to have, but then we get urges from our flesh and end up going back to the very thing that we struggled with. In John 8:36 NLT, Jesus says, *"So if the son sets you free, you are free indeed."* When we truly begin to realize the power of the blood Jesus and what he did for us on the cross, there will be no more failures and relapses. It took me so long to truly realize that I am set free by Jesus, and nothing can change that, except me and my choices.

I can personally tell you, when God delivers you from something, it is very important that we try our best to depend on him so we can stay away from the thing that he has freed us from. It is much harder to find deliverance a second or even third time than it was first time. Why is this? Because when we fall back into our addictions or any bad habit, the shame that the enemy throws at us is heavy, and we can't carry it. It will push us into a dark and alone place where we stop spending time with God, whether that be with prayer or the study of his word. We will begin to think that we have failed God, that we are not good enough for him, that something is wrong with us, and that now we are too far gone for God to forgive us or to love us.

All these thoughts start from the choice to go back to that thing that God has delivered us from. My question to you is, why do you go back? Why is it hard for you to stay away from the thing that you know is harmful to you, not only spiritually, but also physically and mentally? Does it feel good to you? Does it satisfy you? Does it take you away from reality for a temporary period? Take a moment and write these things down. Be honest with yourself so you can talk to God about them and find freedom/healing. Doing this will get down to the root of the problem instead of the surface of it. Remember, God cannot heal or fix anything that is hidden from him. Yes, he already knows what it is that you are going through, but he wants you to talk to him and invite him into your heart. When you begin to truly recognize and see why you do the things you do, there is freedom in it. When God is trying to heal you or fix what is broken, he never just gets to the surface of problems. *God will always get to the root of a problem and end it, if we let him.*

It does not matter if this is your second time or one hundredth time coming to God about an issue or a problem that you may be struggling with; he will always want to fix it and restore you because you are his child. When we allow God to have access to the root of a problem, that is where true healing comes from. I'll put it this way: Imagine you're a gardener and you're trying to uproot a crop or plant that has gone bad. Just picking off the leaves or even the stems would not do much. Over time, the plant would grow back to how it was before you just picked the leaves and stems off. But if you were to get down in the soil and uproot it, the plant would now be dead and couldn't grow back.

It is the same thing with God when we present him our problems. When he begins to get down in the dirt and at the root of problems and brokenness and begins to uproot the reasons why we do certain things, they will not grow back like they have been for the past few days, weeks, months, or even years. As a matter of fact, as he uproots our issues and heals us, he will begin to show us how he can use it for his glory. The fact of the matter is Christian life is not always going to be sunshine and butterflies. There will be failures and setbacks, there will be seasons when it looks like you are at the end, or old habits may resurface, and prayers that you are crying out to him do not get answered instantly. When these things happen, it so important that we do not turn away and run from God because we think he is mad at us. I can personally tell you running away from God or turning your back on him does nothing but make the problems we are facing worse. He is the only who can fix it; he is the only one who can reverse our problems for good, he is the only one where we can find peace in the midst of problems, he is the only one who can uproot problems.

I strongly believe that when we sin or mess up, he comes to us and not turn away from us. I know that sounds weird and different from a lot of our theology, but think about the story of Adam and Eve in the beginning of time. God gave Adam a commandment to not eat the fruit of the tree in the middle of the garden. But sure enough, as we all know, they ended up eating it and did not do what God said. They then hid from God in shame because they knew what they did was wrong. But look at how our Father responded to Adam. In Genesis 3:9 NLT, it says, *"Then the Lord God responded to the man 'where are you?'" God did not turn his back on Adam nor ignore him; he came to Adam because he knew he sinned and didn't do what God told him to do.*

It is the same with us! God comes to us when we sin, not turn away from us. He loves us way too much to turn his back on us when we mess up. Today rest in the fact that God is not mad at you, but he is coming to you with love and compassion. *I want all of us to realize that when we do sin and mess up, he is not mad at us. He is mad at the sin because God does not like sin. He wants to help us with our sin issues, not tear us down.* Yes, our sin has consequences, and he will correct us, but God, in his love, grace, mercy and forgiveness, accepts us as we are and will clean us up in the way that he wants to. But it first requires us to take down the wall of doubt and shame so he can. Today and at this moment, could you let down the walls and let him in? Do not think about what has been and what is. Focus on what will be and the goodness of God. I personally want to encourage you to trust him and to not doubt his presence in your life. I want you to experience freedom and life, but most importantly, God does and he is waiting for you right now as we speak.

I hope this chapter encouraged you to stop going back to old habits and ways that God has set you free from, and I pray that you begin to realize that through Jesus Christ, you truly are free. I am praying for you.

Prayer: Heavenly Father, help me realize that through my acceptance of Jesus Christ as my personal Lord and Savior, I truly am set free. Help me trust the sacrifice that your Son did for me on the cross. And I ask if I do mess up or fall, that you always come to me with love and compassion and teach me where I went wrong. I let go and I trust you. In Jesus name, Amen.

Chapter Seventeen

HEALING OF SCARS

When it comes to finding healing of our scars through Jesus Christ, it is a process. Healing never comes over night. I would love to tell you that when I gave my life to Jesus, all my problems instantly went away, and I became a 100 percent different person the next day. But in reality, those things do not happen. I still would fail, I would stumble every day, and I would still indulge in my addictions. I battled for so long even after giving my life to Jesus. If that is you today, rest in the fact that healing is never going to come or happen overnight. I want all of us to realize that healing and growth is a continuous day-to-day process until Jesus Christ returns. We will never have all the answers or our life figured out. We were never meant to; if we did, that would mean that we wouldn't need God and that we would be just fine without him.

If you are currently in a broken state or don't see the results that you have been praying for, don't lose heart. In Psalms 147:3 NLT, it says, *"God heals the brokenhearted and binds up our wounds."* Today I want you to realize that the God of the universe is eagerly wanting to heal you and bind up all your scars that you have experienced. But how does he do that? God can only heal us and fix the things that we are going through if we spend time with him through prayer and reading of his word on a daily basis. In Romans 12:2 NLT, it says, *"Be transformed by the renewing of your mind."* Healing and transformation do not come from our own power or own will. If that were the case, we would have been healed a long time ago. The healing and transformation that all of us long for and want only comes from the Lord. Yes, we may find temporary healing in ourselves, but permanent healing only comes from God. When we begin to really spend time with God on a day-to-day basis, we begin to know his truth. And when we begin to know the truth, the truth will set us free (John 8:32: NLT). Who is the truth? As we stated earlier in this book, the truth is Jesus Christ. When we begin to know Jesus, he always has a way of healing us the only way that he can do it. The thing is it requires us to trust him and to accept what he did on the cross for us. The problem with a lot of us, including myself, for a long time, shame gets the best of us. *How can we really trust him if we are constantly living in shame every day?* I want to talk about five facts that God says about you that I want you to start saying to yourself every day.

Fact no. 1: I am accepted. I want all of us to realize that the God of the universe has accepted us in Jesus Christ. No matter how messed up or down bad we think we are or how jacked up we see ourselves, God has accepted us in Jesus. In Ephesians 1:6 NLT, it says, *"For the same love he has for is Beloved One, Jesus, he has for us.* And this unfolding plan brings him great pleasure!" How amazing is this news to us? God loves us the same as he loves Jesus. Why? Because before we are anything in this world, before our mess-ups, wrong paths, bad choices, and sin, we are a son or daughter of the Most High God. Not only does God the Father accept us, but Jesus Christ himself also has accepted us. In Romans 15:7 NLT, it says, "Therefore accept each other *just as Christ has accepted you* so that God will be given glory." This just got even more amazing, right? Both God the Father and God the Son accept us as we are in his adopted family. It cannot get better than that. I don't know about you, but this, to me, is mind-blowing.

The perfect sovereign God who stands outside of time accepts us for who we are, not based on what we do, but based on who he is and what Jesus did on the cross. So what happens when our problems have gotten so bad that our friends, coworkers, Bible study group, or even parents stop accepting us? What happens when the people in our lives turn their back on us and aren't there for us? In Psalms 27:10 NLT, it says, *"Even if my father and mother abandon me, the Lord will hold me close."* So not only does God accept us as we are, but he will also stay with us, even if our parents or anyone else in our lives leave us. The faithfulness of God cannot be matched, and he will never not be faithful to you. Today rest in the fact that God accepts you as you are and wants you to have a relationship with him.

Fact no. 2: I am valuable. The fact of the matter is all of us are valuable to God as his children. We may not feel like it, we may not feel worthy or even qualified to be valuable to God, but we are. We are made in his image and his likeness; we are the head and not the tail, we are joint heirs of Christ, we are children of the Most High God, we are royal priests, we are his masterpieces. In Psalms 8:4-5 NLT, it says, "What are mere mortals that you should think about them, human beings that you should care for them? *Yet you made them only a little lower than God and crowned them with glory and honor."* We are literally made just under God. I want you to see how valuable you truly are in the eyes of God; you're not what you call yourself, your struggle, the sin you battle with, the addiction, or the mental bondage that you may experience. In Luke 12:24 NLT, Jesus says, *"God feeds the birds and you are far more valuable to him than any birds!"* Imagine everything that God made. He made the grass in the fields; the waters of the oceans; everything that creeps, crawls, or slithers; the fish in the sea; the animals on land; the humidity of the clouds; and the precipitation that occurs when it rains. He takes care of all those things to make sure everything is in order, right? If the Bible is telling us that we are just below him and we are more valuable than the birds in the sky, why, for another second, should we worry and create an ulcer in our stomach, wondering if we are valuable to God? In Isaiah 43:4 NLT, God says, *"You are precious to me. You are honored and I love you.*" Today I want to encourage you to begin seeing your value through the lenses of God and not through your own lenses. When you begin to see yourself through the lenses of God, everything changes, and you begin to walk with a certain confidence that cannot be broken.

Fact no. 3: I am lovable. Yes, you, the person who battles with an addiction to a substance, the person with lust issues, the person with anxiety, the person with low self-esteem, the person who has anger issues, the person who has failed at something—you are lovable. I don't think we fully understand the depth of God's love for us. God is not a human, so he cannot love by human standards. The love that God shows us is a supernatural unearthly love. In Isaiah 54:10 NLT, it says, "Though the mountains be shaken and the hills be removed, *yet my unfailing love for you will not be shaken nor my covenant of peace removed.* Says the Lord, who has compassion on you." God loves you consistently, and he loves you unconditionally. Remember, earlier in this book, we talked about there being nothing that can separate us from the love of God? There is literally nothing in this world or anything you do that will separate you from his love. God promised that, and he is not a God that he shall lie. I want you to realize that the God of the universe loves you way beyond you can even fathom. His love for you is so deep that it will move you to tears and bring you to your knees. Personally, there have been times when I truly have realized his love for me, and it pushed me into tears. I want you to personally experience that love and feel his loving presence in your life. There is no need to be afraid of what could happen to you or opening up to him because he loves you so much. In Daniel 10:19 NLT, it says, "Don't be afraid, for you are very precious to God. Peace! Be encouraged! Be Strong!" Today I want you to rest in the fact that God loves you beyond words, and he wants you to accept his never-ending love for you.

Fact no. 4: I am forgivable. This fact alone should give all of us a sense of peace and a sense of freedom. You are not too far gone for God to forgive. I don't care what you've done up until this point; you are forgiven by God because of what Jesus did for the cross for you. Do not listen to the devil and the lies he is whispering in your ear. I personally want you to tell the devil to shut up. As a matter of fact, tell the devil that I said that he shut up. When you believed and accepted Jesus Christ as your personal Lord and Savior, the debt of your past sins, current sins, and future sins was paid for. Jesus literally nailed all your sins to the cross two thousand years ago. He knew no sin but became sin because he loved you that much. So when God sees you, he does not see your sin; he sees a child who has believed and accepted his Son Jesus Christ into their hearts. In Isaiah 43:25 NLT, God says, *"I, yes, I alone will blot out your sins for my own sake and will never think of them again."* So not only does God forgive your sins, *but he also chooses to forget your sins.* The blood of Jesus is so powerful that it cleanses your sins forever. You are proven not guilty in the eyes of God if you have accepted Jesus. The thing about this is, before God even made the world, he wanted us to be without fault. In Ephesians 1:4 NLT, it says, *"Even before he made the world, God loved us and chose us in Christ to be holy and without fault in his eyes."* God wanted all of us before we even wanted him. He was thinking about us before we even thought about him. Just think about this for just a second. In the beginning of time, the Holy Trinity (Father, Son, and Holy Spirit) literally had a meeting and chose us and wanted us to be without fault. So when you believe and accept Jesus, you now have obtained the very thing that God wanted you to have from the very beginning. Today I want you to rest in the fact that you are forgivable, no matter what you have done or where you have been.

Fact no. 5: I am capable. You are capable of being healed. You are capable of being restored. You are capable of beating your addiction. You are capable of becoming everything God has called you to be. If you are in the presence of God and you spend time with him, you are beyond capable because you have the God of the universe on your side. In Philippians 4:12 AMP, it says, *"I have strength for all things in Christ who empowers me. I'm ready for anything and equal to anything through him who infuses inner strength into me. That is, I am self-sufficient in Christ sufficiency."* All of us have to the power to do the will of God in this life and the power to beat any type of addiction, chain, or bondage.

We have the Spirit of God that lives inside of us, which gives us a supernatural power. We can either quit when the going gets tough or we can roll up our sleeves and push through it with Jesus while having tears in our eyes. Our self-esteem comes from one or two places in this world: what others say about us or sometimes even ourselves or what God says about us. Who are you going to believe? He will turn your beauty to ashes, and he will not stop chasing you down and loving you. I pray this chapter helped you trust God with your life and begin the healing process. I am praying for you.

Prayer: Heavenly Father, today I want to be healed fully. I want true healing that can only come from you and not from what I can do for myself. Help me realize that I am accepted, valuable, lovable, forgivable, and capable to you. Change me only like you can. I trust you. In Jesus's name, Amen.

Printed in the United States
By Bookmasters